CENTERED IN
GOD

CENTERED IN
GOD

THE WAY OF JESUS
THE WAY OF LIFE

Evan Drake Howard

Augsburg
MINNEAPOLIS

CENTERED IN GOD
The Way of Jesus, The Way of Life

Scripture quotations from the New Revised Standard Version Bible, copyright © 1989 by the Division of Christian Education of the National Council of the Churches of Christ in the U.S.A.

Cover and Text Design: Lois Stanfield, LightSource Images

Library of Congress Cataloging-in-Publication Data

Howard, Evan Drake, 1955–
    Centered in God : the way of Jesus, the way of life / by Evan
Drake Howard : foreword by John Sanford.
        p.   cm.
    Includes bibliographical references.
    ISBN 0-8066-2820-0 (alk. paper)
    1. Jesus Christ—Meditations. 2. Christian life—Metitations.
I. Title.
BT306.5.H685 1995
232—dc20   95-24261
                                                                  CIP

The paper used in this publication meets the minimum requirements of American National Standard for Information Sciences—Permanence of Paper for Printed Library Materials, ANSI Z329.48-1984.

Manufactured in the U.S.A.   AF 9-2820

99   98   97   96   95   1   2   3   4   5   6   7   8   9   10

To Evan John Howard
born June 24, 1994

May he make the way of Jesus his way of life

CONTENTS

FOREWORD

In this well-written book, Evan Drake Howard uses the best of contemporary depth psychology to illuminate the ever powerful teachings of Jesus. But it is not only what Jesus said that we meet in this book, we meet Jesus himself. For not only does Rev. Howard have a good knowledge of psychology and Scripture, but he also shows an intimate knowledge of the Lord.

Howard also uses, sparingly but effectively, examples from his own life and inner experience to give to the reader a feeling of being in immediate touch with him. The impression we get of the author is that he is a man of humility, learning, and an insight gained in part through his own struggle with himself.

Lively quotations are sprinkled throughout this book, from sources, including the Bible, depth psychologists Carl Jung and Fritz Kunkel, and the author's own wife, Carol.

This book should prove helpful to people as a devotional manual and as an aid in forging a new spirituality based on the best of modern depth psychology and, above all, on what Jesus taught and who Jesus was.

JOHN A. SANFORD

PREFACE

I wrote this book as a response to two of the most difficult years of my life. A move to the Chicago area caused much of the difficulty. I started writing after returning to New England, my adopted home, ecstatic about living in Providence, Rhode Island, and serving as pastor of Central Baptist Church. On September 15, 1988, I had been in the city just two days. I went to my new office on that gentle Thursday evening to work on my first sermon—"Together Toward Hope."

I left my office just after 9:30 P.M. In the parking lot, I opened my car door. Turning to my right, I noticed a young woman slumped motionless behind the steering wheel of one of the two other cars in the lot. Fear gripped me. I prayed nothing was wrong, but I knew that there was. I went over and knocked on the car's windshield. No response. I knocked on the window of the door on the driver's side. No response. When I reached to open the door, I suspected that the woman was unconscious, though she was having sporadic seizures. What followed were twenty of the most traumatic minutes of my life.

Alone with the unconscious woman in the darkness of the church parking lot, I was seized by the terror of a nightmare come true. I fought the temptation to panic and drew on first-aid skills learned as a lifeguard during college. Beginning mouth-to-mouth resuscitation, I yelled for help between breaths. For the next seven to ten minutes—an eternity—no one heard. I kept breathing into the woman's lungs, hoping against hope that she would respond. Questions raced through my mind: Who was this woman? How did she end up in our parking lot? What was her story?

The woman was young, attractive, nicely dressed, and drove a car that looked almost new. Whatever her identity, I represented her last hope for life. Vomiting and gasping for breath, she struggled to survive. Neighbors and the police finally arrived, followed by an ambulance. I thought she had a chance.

Later, at the hospital, I learned of her death. I was stunned when the emergency-room physician told me the cause. I thought the woman had had an epileptic seizure, a heart attack, or some other natural physical crisis. Instead, she died of an overdose of sleeping pills and antidepressants. She had taken her own life.

The news of the suicide grieved me. I felt a bond with this woman whom I had never known, but whose life had intersected with mine. I decided that night to write this book, because her tragic death represented more than one woman's defeat. For me, it represented all the pain others had shared with me as a pastor. Her defeat also spoke poignantly to my own pain.

The suicide came at the end of those two difficult years in my life. The difficulty began when I left a pastorate of nearly six years in Cambridge, Massachusetts, to take a half-time job as a chaplain at the University of Chicago. We moved when my wife and I decided that she should accept a position offered to her in Illinois. Carol's job became primary.

I was perplexed by the changing roles of men and women, and I found it hard to fit the mold of today's liberated husband. Having to subordinate my career to my wife's threatened my sense of masculine identity. Internal voices called on me to be strong as well as vulnerable, head of the household as well as interdependent spouse. I was not internally secure enough to meet these expectations.

In addition, my half-time job discouraged me. I felt disoriented in a new environment and daunted by the pressure to renew a dormant ministry. I longed for community with others but didn't find it in a competitive atmosphere where few students participated in the program I offered. Money problems also weighed on my mind, as did my unfinished doctoral thesis. The hour spent commuting in the morning and evening intensified my sense of aloneness and fatigue, especially when driving through a Chicago ghetto or when stuck in an expressway traffic jam.

I felt crushed. Meanwhile, the demands and politics of Carol's job were also becoming unmanageable. After much thought and struggle, we decided to leave the area. My search for a new pastorate deepened my crisis. I found the placement process emotionally draining; it reduced me to tears on more than one occasion. Tears were my response not only to the uncertainty I felt, but also to the hopes that had died, the relationships that had failed, the confidence I had lost. It seemed so unfair. Life's agonizing paradoxes and debilitating hurts overwhelmed me.

I wrote this book because the woman's suicide and my brush with brokenness led me to re-examine my faith. I saw how superficial my spirituality was, particularly when compared with the spirituality of Jesus Christ, which sprang from his depths. Having encountered the writings of the Swiss psychiatrist Carl Gustav Jung as part of my doctoral program at Boston University, I rediscovered the power of these writings to illuminate Jesus' experience as well as my own. Jung's depth psychology can be summarized in two words: "Know thyself." Entering into this self-knowledge is what he called becoming conscious, an important part of enhancing one's freedom and gaining greater control of one's life.

With the help of Jung's interpreters, including Fritz Kunkel, John A. Sanford, Robert A. Johnson, and Morton Kelsey, I found renewal in following Jesus through the stages of his faith development as presented in the Gospels. That's what this book is about. It attempts to integrate depth psychology with Christian spirituality. Nurturing this integration within, I believe, enables one to become "centered in God."

Jesus' life and message, as well as the teachings of Jung and his followers, invite us into this centeredness through the transformation of our inner lives. This transformation requires that we imitate Jesus as well as believe in him. His spirituality unites faith with practice, prayer with ethics, the mind with the heart, the body with the soul, the past with the present and the future. The possibility of being transformed by sharing his inner life offers hope in good times and bad. It comforts me when I am disturbed, and it disturbs me when I am comfortable. It helps me to claim my personhood and rest in grace.

Centeredness is nurtured by integrative love, Christ's unique gift. He loved God, others, and self as a unity. These three distinct yet intertwined relationships became one in his life. To imitate him is to maximize love's potential. It is to share in the peace and power of his profound inner harmony. As we express love Godward, outward, and inward, we experience the spiritual intimacy that Jesus experienced. This intimacy evokes what the Quaker teacher Thomas R. Kelly calls "serenity, unshakableness, firmness of life-orientation."[1]

This is what I call centeredness; it overflows into the world in acts of justice, compassion, and healing. Without integrative love, chaos results. Somalia and the former Soviet Union, Northern Ireland and South Africa, Bosnia and the Middle East—these are all examples of chaos in other parts of the world. But chaos also lurks close to home. It invades the relationships of dysfunctional families and fuels the violence in America's cities. It simmers in the hearts of the addicted and festers in the minds of the bored and the broken.

An incongruity exists between this turmoil and the abundant life God promises. Can a resolution be found? Are personal and social healing real possibilities or merely dreams? Since the Thursday night of my first week in Providence, I have often asked these questions. I invite you to explore with me an approach to faith that offers some new answers.

Although nothing can bring back the woman who died in the parking lot of Central Baptist Church, I hope our search will help others to avoid her plight. To this day, it unnerves me to think that while I was in my office, writing a sermon entitled "Together Toward Hope," she sat in desperation in her car, right outside my window, ending her life.

I wish she had seen my light and knocked on the door. She didn't. This book is my attempt to give you the spiritual support I could not give her. You will find this support when faith *in* Jesus and the faith *of* Jesus intersect in your heart. This *centering faith* not only overcomes despair—it also creates joy and sends ordinary people into the world as agents of hope and peace. I cannot promise that this faith will solve all of your problems. It has not solved all of mine. But it *has* positively changed my life and helped me weather many crises since September 1988.

I offer no quick fixes. I cannot even guarantee that having found centering faith, you won't lose it again. Such guarantees misrepresent the nature of the inward quest. The quest depends on you. Making progress requires not only spiritual discipline but also a keen awareness of your feelings, wounds, and needs.

This much I know: When you are centered in God, nothing can shake your stability. Centeredness becomes the knot at the end of your rope. Centeredness keeps you hanging on when tough relationships dangle you over a treacherous emotional precipice. It saves your sanity when you're under stress at home, school, or work. Amid sickness or sorrow, trauma or tragedy, fear or failure, loneliness or loss, centeredness will hold you; it won't let you fall. It's strong and resilient enough to support you even in death.

I hope the promise of being centered in God comes alive for you in the pages ahead. Believing this promise, you open yourself to inner growth; sharing this promise, you ensure that the woman who took her life in the church parking lot will not have died in vain. Come with me now as we seek this promise together.

EVAN DRAKE HOWARD

FOLLOW YOUR BLISS, BUT MAKE SURE IT'S REAL

The Challenge of Imitation

> *They were on the road, going up to Jerusalem, and Jesus was walking ahead of them; and they were amazed.*
>
> MARK 10:32

In a conversation with Bill Moyers on PBS, the mythologist Joseph Campbell recalled a scene he had encountered in a restaurant. He was seated next to a family of three and overheard them arguing. The father said to his twelve-year-old son, "Drink your tomato juice." When the boy refused, the father raised his voice and repeated the command, "Drink your tomato juice!"

Again, defiance. Two stubborn wills were deadlocked; the mother had to intervene. She said to her husband, "Don't make him do what he doesn't want to do."

The father retorted, "He can't go through life doing what he wants to do. If he does only what he wants to do, he'll be dead. Look at me. I've never done a thing I wanted to in all my life."

Campbell emphasized the mistake the father had made: He had never "followed his bliss."[1] I am intrigued by Campbell's phrase. The idea of following my bliss appeals to me; it also confuses me, however, because I am not sure how to do this. What does it mean to follow your bliss? Where does one begin?

Perhaps these are your questions, too. Think of your most ecstatic moments, the times when you tasted the bliss of life's goodness. You felt peaceful and thankful and joyful. A sense of rapture welled up within you, a rapture you wanted to last forever.

When did this occur? Maybe you felt bliss a long time ago, when you were a child running across an open meadow, riding a bike for the first time, or swimming with your friends on a hot summer's day. Then again, maybe you experienced bliss more recently. Bliss surprised you in a moment of creative activity. It startled you when you got a job promotion, greeted you on your wedding day, or dazzled you in the glory of a sunset.

The problem with such moments is that they never last. Bliss is as fickle as a spurned lover: it frustrates all suitors. That's why we turn to religion for help. Most religions try to describe what bliss is and how to experience it again; Christianity is no different.

TOWARD INTEGRATIVE FAITH

The gospel proclaims Jesus Christ as the way to bliss. He died to free us from sin and guilt; he rose again to defeat death and offer us eternal life. Christianity celebrates grace. It declares that we can be transformed: made new! Communion with God today, bliss in eternity—this is what faith in Christ promises.

The problem is that when I am at the end of my rope, the promise of future bliss rings hollow. I am sure God has abandoned me. I feel alone, disillusioned, broken, and find no solace in future promises. These promises seem so unreal that they increase my anguish.

Versions of Christianity that emphasize future bliss more than present coping skills are not realistic enough to hold me up amid life's turbulence. A fragmented gospel that understates the role of struggle in the spiritual quest only increases my anxiety.

Integration of belief and experience is needed. Accepting grace is not enough; one must practice grace, as Jesus did. Imitating him helps us experience bliss as an unshakable centeredness right now, and as a promised ecstasy in the future. Centeredness becomes possible when faith *in* Jesus is integrated with the faith *of* Jesus.

We sense a depth in Jesus not found in anyone else. In the early years of this century, the German theologian Rudolf Otto described this depth as the *numinous presence.*[2] Those around Jesus felt something powerful in him, as if they were experiencing another world. The Gospel of Mark says of the disciples, "They were on the road, going up to Jerusalem, and Jesus was walking ahead of them; and they were amazed" (Mark 10:32).

New Testament scholar Marcus J. Borg sees a link between Jesus' spirituality and a vital Christian life today. As a Jew, Jesus almost certainly worshiped in the synagogue every Sabbath, and perhaps on Mondays and Thursdays as well. He would have recited the *Shema* at the beginning and end of each day, affirming with all Jews: "Hear O Israel: The Lord our God is the Lord alone; and you shall love the Lord your God with all your heart, and with all your soul, and with all your might" (Deut. 6:4–5). The gospels bear witness to his mastery of the Hebrew Scriptures. He probably sang the psalms on pilgrimages to Jerusalem and also participated in the Jewish festivals.[3] Borg contends that Jesus' experience of the Spirit is the key to understanding his message and impact on history. Jesus not only believed in God; he actually knew God. At some point in his life, he must have embarked on a religious quest. We know this because he left conventional life behind and became a follower of John the Baptist in his late twenties or around the age of thirty. It is likely that this quest resulted in an enlightenment experience similar to those reported by other great sages.[4]

Jesus was in the charismatic tradition of Judaism. This is the tradition of prophets such as Moses, Elijah, and Ezekiel, who saw into the other world through the eyes of their souls. At his baptism Jesus had a similar vision as the Spirit descended on him. An inner attentiveness empowered his life and ministry. It is likely that he developed this attentiveness through contemplative prayer. He communed with God in long periods of solitude, as did the Galilean holy men and Jewish mystics of his day. "In the morning, while it was still very dark," reports Mark, Jesus "got up and went out to a deserted place, and there he prayed" (Mark 1:35). Luke tells of the crowds that swarmed around him to be healed of their diseases only to find that "he would withdraw to deserted places and pray" (Luke 5:16). On occasion he prayed all night (Luke 6:12).

Such lengthy periods of solitude do not imply verbal prayer but an entry into deeper levels of consciousness through meditation. By stilling the mind and directing the heart toward God, one invites the spiritual intimacy that fosters peace. That Jesus knew this intimacy is suggested by his use of the word *Abba* to address God. In English, *Abba* is translated "Daddy" or "Papa" and is a departure from the more formal "Father" used in traditional Judaism. The intimacy of this word dramatizes the intensity of Jesus' spirituality and his identification with the charismatic tradition of his time. No wonder the disciples sometimes observed a renewed vitality and power in him when he returned from periods of meditation.[5]

Jesus' teachings flowed from his experience of God. His teaching radically criticized the conventional wisdom of his time, which honored family and wealth, power and achievement, religious observance and social status. He invited his followers to undertake an inward journey that would result in personal transformation and social reform. This journey involves centering one's heart in God. Such centering is the opposite as well as the antidote to anxiety; it is what Jesus meant by faith.[6]

Jesus' experience of the Spirit convinced him that God is gracious and compassionate. This challenged the image of God as judge that dominated the thinking of his day. Rather than establishing boundaries and enforcing the requirements of conventional wisdom, the God whom Jesus knew loves all people, including sinners and outcasts. Calling God "compassionate" resonates deeply in Hebrew and Aramaic, in which the word is the plural of "womb." God is "wombish"—tender, nourishing, comforting, life-giving.[7] The good news of Jesus' message, says Borg, "leads from a life of anxiety to a life of peace and trust. It leads from the bondage of self-preoccupation to the freedom of self-forgetfulness. It leads from life centered in culture to life centered in God."[8]

More than anyone else who has ever lived, Jesus practiced the presence of God and explored his own inner depths. Rivers of serenity surged in him, fed by his union with the divine. Such are the possibilities that await us if we become centered in his spirituality. Though each day presents us with challenges and struggles, Jesus goes ahead of us, illuminating a path that guides us to integrative love—if we follow in his steps (Peter 2:21).

FINDING THE RIGHT RHYTHM

Jesus' inner journey toward bliss is a parable of our own journey of the soul. He experienced all that brings us to the end of our rope, but the depth of his spirituality was the knot that kept him hanging on. Turmoil in his family, hunger in the wilderness, exhaustion in his work, opposition from his enemies, betrayal by a friend, death by crucifixion—he endured all of this and more. Yet these experiences increased his awareness of God instead of diminishing it. This is because the rhythm of his life alternated between active contemplation and contemplative action. Grounded in integrative love, he became all we are meant to be—people in touch with the *numinous presence* in every moment.

In her classic study of mysticism, theologian Evelyn Underhill observed that the spiritual masters of many traditions have seen in Jesus' life the soul's journey toward bliss. The soul's awareness of God is born weak and fragile. It grows through poverty and temptation, solitude and surrender; it deepens through service and contemplation. Crisis intrudes in the "dark night," when the soul feels abandoned by the divine. By persevering in faith, the soul is transfigured in resurrection, glorified in union with God.

This was Jesus' experience. Underhill identifies five stages of the journey toward bliss: awakening, purgation, illumination, dark night of the soul, and union.[9] Jesus had an *awakening* of his Christ consciousness at his baptism. Through the *purgation* of his spirit in the wilderness, he learned the discipline of patient attentiveness. His *illumination* occurred on the Mount of Transfiguration; his *dark night of the soul*, in the garden and on the cross. Easter celebrates his resurrection and *union* with God.

Psychologist Carl Jung used the term *individuation* to describe the growth one attains by imitating Jesus' spiritual journey. In simplest terms, individuation is the process of becoming complete and whole as a person. It involves bringing into consciousness the unconscious aspects of one's being. Becoming your own unique self requires reconciling the opposites within you until you are at one with yourself. This process ordinarily cannot begin until the second half of life.

Individuation is an arduous journey undertaken by few. Those who do undertake it and persevere in its disciplines forge a balance between their individuality and their relationship to others. They live creatively from their inner center of wholeness and achieve the self-transcendence essential to well-being.

The goal of individuation is the realization of the Self (what Christians call the image of God within us). The *self* is also Jung's term for the organizing center of the personality, the unifying principle in each person that bears the imprint of divinity. The self is an archetype, a model of psychological functioning that is intangible yet from which clear patterns of meaning and behavior emerge. As a potentiality at the core of one's being, the self is the source of hidden possibilities, desires, aspirations, values, and attitudes. It embraces both the conscious and the unconscious. [10]

Another important component of the psyche is the ego. Whereas the self is born, the ego is made. It comes into being through human growth and development. The ego is the center of conscious life, the part of the personality we project to others. The self may be called "the mover" and the ego "the moved," but ideally they are interdependent. When properly related to the self, the ego responds creatively to the demands of life. But when egocentric—that is, alienated from the self—the ego's responses are stilted and unproductive. [11]

The spiritual quest can illuminate one's awareness of these intricate psychic relationships. Bringing one's depths into consciousness evokes the self-knowledge that produces centeredness. This is what Jesus achieved through his spirituality of integrative love. [12]

I identify with Jesus because he was as human as I am. He knew the terror of life's adversity, but he overcame fear with faith. This is also our challenge; it requires practice as well as belief. The imitation of Christ begins with an acknowledgment of our weakness. By bringing our inner alienation into the light of consciousness, we transcend our unhealthy responses to it and overcome self-defeating behaviors.

NO ROOM FOR SPECTATORS

You and I were created for communion with God. By communion I don't mean attendance at Sunday worship or weekly prayer meetings, as commendable as these are. I am talking about a moment-by-moment sense of God's presence, a pervasive spiritual attentiveness from which power and love emerge.

The imitation of Christ nurtures this attentiveness; passive faith stifles it. Casting oneself in the role of observer, not participant in the spiritual life, is confining. Two men I know were single at midlife. Both wanted to be married, but neither had found the right woman. Both were handsome, successful professionals, but they disagreed about how to find a mate. One of them joined several clubs and took up square dancing. He eventually married a woman he met at one of these social events. The other man felt it would be inauthentic for him to take any intentional steps to find a wife. He is still single.

If we remain passive, as the second man did, we miss opportunities for intimacy with God. This is a particular problem for those of us who grew up in the church. We often substitute dead religion for living faith. The gospel sounds ordinary because we have heard it so many times. We may find meaning in religious rituals but have little awareness of God in our daily routine. Such shallowness cannot evoke wonder or awe. Neither can it call us to service, comfort us in perplexity, nor sustain us in crisis. This passivity is what Anglican bishop Michael Marshall calls "decaffeinated Christianity": it promises not to keep us awake at night.

We crave integration. Hope for finding it lies in reclaiming our sense of self through a growing spiritual awareness. In the fifteenth-century devotional classic, *The Imitation of Christ,* Thomas à Kempis says of this awareness, "If just once you could perfectly enter the inner life of Jesus and experience a little of his passionate love, then you would not care at all about what you might gain or lose in life. . . . A lover of Jesus and of truth, a genuinely spiritual person who is free from a troubled heart, can turn himself to God at any time, rise above himself, and rest joyfully in the Lord." [13]

Let me be clear: I don't believe anyone can imitate Jesus on her or his own. To try to do so reduces Christianity to a religion of works, not grace. We need both qualities. The gospel calls us to salvation in Christ, but also to transformed living. *How* we believe is as crucial as *what* we believe. As Martin Luther said, "It is not imitation which brings about our sonship [or daughtership] of God but our sonship [or daughtership] which makes possible imitation." [14] Having received God's unconditional acceptance through faith in the crucified and risen Christ, we grow spiritually by practicing the faith of the human Jesus. The discipline of imitation sustains, nurtures, and deepens the new birth of conversion.

This discipline involves turning inward regularly, as Jesus did. As we imitate him in cultivating mindfulness, we have reverence for the God who reverences us. We no longer feel alone or afraid, but rest in mercy, peace, and acceptance. We are "quickened into quietness," to use Thomas R. Kelly's phrase.[15]

A NEW WAY OF COPING

Solitude connects us with the quiet center within; it is the place where God dwells and mindfulness grows. From this center we are equipped not only to triumph in adversity but also to see the spiritual meaning of every experience. Even our mundane activities—eating and sleeping, business affairs, household duties, and leisure pursuits—become opportunities to explore the quietness within and express gratitude.

The quietness whets our desire for intimacy with God; imitating Christ advances us toward it. Just believing in him is not enough; he calls us to active faith. He had the ten lepers show themselves to the priest and thereby participate in their healing. He commanded the lame man at the pool of Bethesda to *take up his mat* and walk, to put his faith into practice. Before the man who had been born blind could be healed, he first had to wash in the pool of Siloam.

Jesus' own faith was not passive but passionate, as some of his startling statements show. He urges us to "say to this mountain, 'Be taken up and thrown into the sea,' and if you do not doubt in your heart, . . . it will be done for you" (Mark 11:23). He states, "If you had faith the size of a mustard seed, you could say to this mulberry tree, 'Be uprooted, . . . and it would obey you" (Luke 17:6). Those who believe, as Jesus did, receive what they ask for in prayer (Mark 11:24). Whatever they bind on earth will be bound in heaven; whatever they loose on earth will be loosed in heaven (Matt. 18:18).

Integrating faith *in* Jesus with the faith *of* Jesus enables one to participate in the wholeness of God. As we follow the man from Nazareth in spiritual discipline, we share in the paradox of his human divinity and divine humanity. Making his faith our own, we are formed in the image of his fully integrated personality.

Faith's call to imitation reminds me of an experience I had as a teenager. My friends and I swam at the local pool. We competed to see who would be the first to dive—not jump—off the ominous high dive. Each of us ascended the ladder and walked onto the board, determined to be the first to accomplish the feat. But each looked down, became afraid, and jumped, humiliated.

Then it was Stan's turn. Stronger and better built than the rest of us, he was always poised under pressure. I admired Stan. More, I believed in him. I watched from below as he climbed the ladder. Once atop the high dive, he took several quick steps, bounced confidently on the end of the board, and dove head-first into the pool.

Now, who would be next? Stan made it look easy; I felt I could do it, too. I lurched up the ladder with iron-fisted determination. Then I looked down. Dizzied by fear, I couldn't go through with it. I jumped. The jeers of my friends greeted me when I surfaced. Believing *in* Stan didn't stop me from embarrassing myself. I needed the faith *of* Stan—the faith that emboldened him to dive head-first.

I feel the same way about being a Christian. I believe in Jesus as my Savior and try to follow him as Lord every day. But this belief neither protects me from, nor enables me to, transcend life's struggles. No matter how passionately I believe *in* Jesus, I can't escape this basic human problem.

But there is a way to cope. As we integrate the risen Lord and his faith into our lives, we become *like* him. We start thinking as he thought and accepting the challenges he accepted. Learning to love as he loved, we become whole in God as he was whole in God.

To follow Christ in integrative faith is to follow your bliss. Not only do you find a new identity in and through him, you also find a resilient centeredness and strength you never knew you had. Discovering integrative faith is like coming to an oasis amid the desert of inner barrenness. The oasis is life at its best—full and rich, abundant and growing, beautiful and free.

Having tasted this richness, you won't want to return to the desert. You'll want to stay at the oasis. You'll want to eat and drink of life's goodness and joy until you are satisfied. But staying at the oasis means being honest about where you need to grow, no matter how painful that may be.

MEDITATION

Sit in a quiet place and allow yourself to relax and become peaceful. Close your eyes and meditate on the words of Jesus: "Truly I tell you, if you say to this mountain, 'Be taken up and thrown into the sea,' and if you do not doubt in your heart, but believe that what you say will come to pass, it will be done for you" (Mark 11:23).

Think about the mountains in your life: the loneliness, anger, exhaustion, or depression that needs to be moved; the self-doubt or disillusionment, emptiness or boredom, shame or fear that undermines your peace; your painful relationships or complex problems. These are all mountains of oppression, as are the social injustices of bigotry, poverty, and war. Meditate on the promise of Jesus that if you have faith and not doubt, you can move these mountains with God's help.

Breathe deeply. With each slow breath, recite one of the following affirmations to yourself until you have repeated all seven:

1. *God is within me.*
2. *God is beside me.*
3. *God is before me.*
4. *God is behind me.*
5. *God is above me.*
6. *God is below me.*
7. *Because God is all around me and within me, I can move mountains.*

Repeat this exercise of breathing and meditation until your mood becomes serene and confident and you feel ready to live out your faith in action.

PRAYER

I pause to listen for your voice,
O God of mystery and might.

You speak words I need to hear—
words of challenge as well as assurance,
words of critique as well as affirmation.

The silence of these moments invites you
into my spirit anew.

I sense your presence in the air I breathe,
the beauty I see,
the quietness I feel within.

My depths are full of you,
O Lover of my soul.

In seeking you,
I follow my bliss;
I journey into unexplored realms
of power and possibility.

Thank you for faith that moves mountains;
may it be mine.

Thank you for walking by my side
and picking me up when I fall.

You are there in my loneliest moments,
my hardest relationships,
my darkest fears.

(continued)

(continued)

You never withdraw from me,
O God of hope and wholeness.

Help me imitate you.

Take me from passivity to involvement,
from slumber to awakening.

May I not be a spectator
but a participant in life,
and may my path find me always
walking in the footsteps of Jesus,
my Lord. Amen.

WHAT YOU SOW IN TRUTH YOU'LL REAP IN GROWTH

The Challenge of Honesty

"Truth above all, even when it upsets and overwhelms us!" These words by the Swiss poet and philosopher Henri Frederic Amiel sound the rallying cry of the inward journey. Amiel is right: Sometimes the truth hurts. That's why spiritual growth can be painful—it involves facing our deepest fears and insecurities. This is a hard lesson that many of us go to extremes to avoid learning.

A man in his early thirties once came to me in anguish. He had an unusual request: that I help him move to another state. "Why do you want to leave?" I asked.

"Because people here are ruining my life," he said. "My parents criticize me, my coworkers ridicule me, my wife left me, and my landlord wants to evict me. People here are mean; I want to make a fresh start somewhere else."

I told him I could understand why he might want to move. It's painful to live with such adversity; sometimes a change of environment does a person good. But I warned him that moving helps only when the adversity is caused by external factors, not internal ones. If alienated within, he would alienate others, anywhere. The scenery would changes, but his problems would remain the same.

After three days they found him in the temple, sitting among the teachers, listening to them and asking them questions. And all who heard him were amazed at his understanding and his answers.

LUKE 2:46–47

When I asked why he thought people were against him, his response revealed the inner nature of his problems: "My mom and dad abused me emotionally when I was growing up but consider themselves good parents. Having me around exposes their hypocrisy; they criticize me to express their resentment. My coworkers resent me, too. They're jealous of my work, so they ridicule me and make my life miserable. As for my ex-wife, she's immature and hateful. And my landlord is greedy; he wants to evict me so he can raise the rent on the next tenant."

"Are you sure you haven't done anything to cause these conflicts?" I asked.

"Are you kidding?" he asked. "These people are vicious. They want to ruin my life!"

When I pressed the matter further, he became agitated. Glaring at me, he shouted, "You're as cruel as they are! You want to ruin me, too!"

I have come to expect anger when I question someone's complaints against another person. There is security in blame, and when I threaten this security, I become the object of the blamer's wrath. The wrath is rooted in denial, the choice to suppress the truth and avoid facing painful inner issues. Psychiatrist Elisabeth Kübler-Ross calls denial a buffer that helps a person cope with disturbing facts. Sometimes this buffer is necessary for survival: it relieves grief. As a long-term solution, however, denial doesn't work. It not only prevents us from finding solutions to our problems, it also makes the problems worse by encouraging unhealthy responses to them.

THE SEEKER'S JOURNEY

The way of transformation is the way of truth. Authentic well-being requires complete honesty. Without honesty, you lose your self-respect. You exhaust yourself trying to maintain a facade. Haunted by something askew in your life, you are afraid to face it, and even more afraid of being exposed as an impostor. So you find sophisticated ways to avoid your real self. This creates inner alienation, plaguing you with nagging guilt. You feel discontent and know that something is wrong, but you are threatened at the prospect of delving deeply to discover what it is. Without courage, your discontent will remain and may turn into depression.

Because he was fully human, Jesus must have fought this battle as well. He could not find integrative love apart from the truth any more than we can. Although he was unique in having come "full of grace and truth" (John 1:14), he was like us in that he also sought the truth amid ambiguity.

His search began in the temple, which Luke tells us he visited at age twelve. On the return journey, his parents discovered him missing. They found him "sitting among the teachers, listening to them and asking them questions. And all who heard him were amazed at his understanding and his answers" (Luke 2:46-47).

This is the first incident in the Gospels that describes Jesus' conscious life. Angels heralded his birth; a dramatic baptism launched his ministry, but sandwiched between these events is this one vignette from his youth. It dramatizes a poignant message: The individuating ego reverences truth; its journey toward completeness begins in the temple of humility.

This experience from his youth set the tone for Jesus' continuing spiritual journey. His disciplined contemplation kindled in him a refreshing authenticity. Having first submitted to God in humility, he spoke with authority. "For this I was born, and for this I came into the world," he told Pilate, "to testify to the truth" (John 18:37). He prefaced many of his statements with the phrase, "I tell you in truth." He even made the claim, "I am . . . the truth" (John 14:6). Such a claim sounds exaggerated, even ludicrous. But as the Christ he would have been dishonest not to have made it.

Jesus never let the consequences deter him from speaking the truth. Echoing the Greek concept of truth as "unhiddenness or unveiling," he declared that "nothing is covered up that will not be uncovered and nothing secret that will not become known" (Matt. 10:26).

He attacked hypocrisy as a betrayal of truth. The scribes and Pharisees deserved criticism because they "tithe mint, dill, and cummin, and have neglected the weightier matters of the law: justice and mercy and faith" (Matt. 23:23). By contrast, both word and deed corresponded in Jesus. He proclaimed grace to the outcasts; therefore he ate with tax collectors and sinners. He was Messiah in word, announcing the Kingdom of God; he was also Messiah in deed, demonstrating the kingdom's advent in works of power.[1]

Jesus declared, "If you continue in my word, you are truly my disciples; and you will know the truth, and the truth will make you free" (John 8:31-32). This statement is about finding spiritual intimacy through deliverance from sin. Such intimacy requires confronting the foibles of our human nature. Grace sustains us in this confrontation; it enables us to live in the freedom of God, who alone is ultimately free.

TAKING OFF THE MASKS

When you acknowledge your dishonesties and evasions, you banish phoniness and become real. You are free to take off your inner masks. Relying on grace, you bring your dark side to God and own it. In Christ, God accepts you just as you are. That's what grace is—the great gift of God's unconditional acceptance. Healed by this deep affirmation of your worth, you integrate your darkness into your self-awareness. You are no longer in denial; you are on your way to awakening. This process requires a willingness to suffer; it demands rigorous introspection and discipline. Sacrifices must be made and attitudes changed if you want to realize your full selfhood.

As a young minister, I had an inflated opinion of my preaching abilities. My need for approval led me to accept positive feedback and deny criticism. My wife, Carol, on the other hand, pointed out where I needed to improve my sermons. Because I was too insecure to hear it, this made Sunday afternoons tense.

Carol knew I would not grow until I became honest with myself, so she found a creative way to help. She listened to my sermons and wrote her impressions on her worship bulletin. She was positive after each service, but she left the bulletin in the house where I would find it. On the back I saw her real comments. Her sharing said, "I love you and I'm for you, but you've got some work to do in this area of ministry."

Years later, as I sat reading those sermons, I finally admitted she was right. Her comments made me face the truth of my mediocre preaching. As a result, I let go of my unrealistic expectations, embraced "pretty good" as good enough, and felt free.

This experience taught me how difficult owning our vulnerabilities can be. When faced with our real selves, we tremble. Sensitive emotions bristle. Fragile egos shatter. Images of what we are scuttle dreams of what we had hoped to become. It hurts. Criticism is threatening and it makes us defensive. If deserved, this criticism forces us to exchange illusions for facts, and this involves grief.

Fear of grief stymies growth. Only by mourning our losses in a healthy way do we grow to accept them. We must grieve the death of false images of ourselves and embrace the true person who arises from the ashes. Therein lies the problem. Many of us would rather remain in denial than do the grief work that honesty requires. The price we pay is a loss of inner integrity.

The problem stems from an improper relationship with what Jung called *persona*. The persona is the face we show to the world; it is the role we play in order to be accepted. The efficient business person, the concerned parent, the eccentric artist, the confident attorney—all are actors on life's stage. So are you and I. We hide behind external appearances, revealing our true selves only to a trusted few. Though often necessary, this causes problems when our self-image is rooted not in who we are but in what we do.

Jung called this "character-splitting."[2] It happens when our persona contradicts our authentic inner identity. Life becomes a role-play, not an expression of one's deeper being, and the self, the real person, cannot emerge. Such repression results in a denial of the rest of the personality. Thus, the revered pastor cannot admit his sexual indiscretions, the self-sacrificing mother her alcoholism, the esteemed professor his arrogance. Such people have not come fully into consciousness; they have over-identified with the persona. Estranged from the truth about themselves, they cannot be free. As American philosopher Eric Hoffer said, "We lie loudest when we lie to ourselves." Deception expands our inner darkness, and we cannot respond to the light of the Spirit.

BREAKING A VICIOUS CYCLE

Getting stuck in denial is oppressive. It makes us victims of unconsciousness, blamers who evade responsibility. Dwelling on how circumstances, other people, or God have hurt us, we deprive ourselves of an honest inner dialogue. Contentment eludes us as we become captives of negative emotions: anger and pride, cynicism and self-pity.

One reason we practice denial is because we want to think highly of ourselves and have others think of us as in control. Our perfectionist culture reinforces this desire. Do you remember the advice of actress Lauren Hutton? "Never *ever* let them see you sweat." But if you have lived through the loss of a job, a divorce, problems with your children, or any major failure, you have sweated plenty. These experiences deepen old self-doubts and create new ones. To be human is to be susceptible to this vicious cycle. To break the cycle you must acknowledge your weakness and develop a strategy to cope. Self-knowledge—facing the truth about yourself—is the place to begin.

In this age of celebrity facades and media illusions, facing truth doesn't come easy. We are not encouraged to feel our real feelings, to be our real selves. Today's role models project an air of invulnerability. The TV news anchor, the self-made entrepreneur, the movie star, or the professional athlete—their lives seem perfect. But that often leaves us trying to appear as "together" as these celebrities *seem* to be. We spend valuable psychic energy suppressing our inadequacies. We bury them within and pretend they don't exist. The result is the feeling of inner alienation.

Denial creates broken environments. Estranged from ourselves, we introduce conflict into society. When I hear about an incident of gay-bashing, wife-beating, or racial violence, I often wonder if the real cause was some threat to the aggressor's inner security. Doubts about one's sexual, social, or racial identity can provoke deadly hostilities. such neurotic responses are enslaving; they deny the real problem, which is fragmented spirituality, the failure to rest in the God who, in the words of theologian Paul Tillich, invites us to "accept the fact that you are accepted." [3]

THE WAY OF DELIVERANCE

Christ's call to interpretive faith is a call to honesty. The call is so universal that it addresses everyone, yet so particular that it comes to you and me as if intended for us alone. He invites us into the union of the soul with God.

Tillich wrote *The Courage to Be* to help people become brave enough to claim their true selves. He contends that one must assert one's personhood against all threats. Do you question your self-worth? Are you afraid of rejection? Do you doubt your social skills, intellectual capabilities, or professional competence? To grow beyond these liabilities, you must acknowledge them and embrace your God-given dignity. This takes the courage that "is self-affirmation 'in-spite-of'—in spite of that which tends to prevent the self from affirming itself."[4]

Without courage there can be no honesty; only the brave face the truth about themselves and life and God. The word *courage* comes from the same stem as the French word *coeur,* meaning "heart." Psychological virtues depend on courage for their development.

True, we preserve our personhood by the quality of our decisions. But if these decisions are going to nurture *being* and *becoming,* they require a moral focus. Psychologist Rollo May has explained that "courage is not a virtue or value among other personal values like love or fidelity. It is the foundation that underlies and gives reality to all other virtues and personal values."[5]

The courage to be honest spurs spiritual growth. Those who start facing their problems head-on often wish they had done it sooner: they regret the years they wasted in avoidance. I know a man who almost lost his job when he got drunk at an office party and made sexual advances toward a woman coworker. The woman charged him with sexual harassment. His employer gave him two alternatives: either enroll in an alcohol-treatment program or get fired. He chose to enter a program and began recovery. Now he attends Alcoholics Anonymous meetings and works on the inner issues that contributed to his addiction. He said to me, "I know it sounds strange, but I'm glad I got charged with sexual harassment. I needed a jolt to make me face my alcoholism. Now I understand my problem and have support for solving it. I'm happier than I've ever been."

This kind of openness and self-realization is rare. Many of us miss similar opportunities for catharsis because we are threatened by the implications of honesty. Being honest means acknowledging our brokenness, becoming vulnerable, and committing ourselves to change. Courage is required. That's what Jesus had. He overcame fear by faith and invites us to do the same. But his version of faith can be dangerous. It made him so genuine that, after three years of prophetic ministry, crucifixion became inevitable.

In a world of illusions, Jesus threatened those in power. They sent Jesus to the cross to discredit him. He refused to retract his teachings or apologize to those he offended by his decisive actions, although doing so might have saved him. His self-giving on the cross declared that truth has a higher value than life itself, empowering and transforming those who revere it.

This reverence begins with the courage to be honest. One must be willing to practice self-confrontation, to ask, "What have the people closest to me said about my idiosyncrasies? Where have they tried to get me to change? Is my conscience telling me anything? Which attitudes or actions of mine bring others pain?"

Listen to your life. Dream work is a good way to do this. Dreams reveal the stirrings of the unconscious. By recording your dreams and reflecting on them over time, you will notice recurring themes. These themes can speak God's truth, giving you insight into yourself and showing you where you need to change or grow. Pay attention to dominant themes, good and bad. Be honest, even when it hurts. This is moral courage, a gift no one but God can give you. Once you receive this gift, you will know the truth, and the truth will make you free.

The Greek word translated "know" here, from John 8:32, is the verbal form of the word *gnosis,* which refers to knowledge learned by intimate experience. "You will *know* the truth," says Jungian analyst John A. Sanford, "means not a mere intellectual knowledge, but a deep inner knowing."[6]

By reverencing the truth in this way, you discover that it's okay to be who you are. It's okay to feel your emotions. It's okay to be strong or weak, happy or sad, peaceful or depressed. It's okay, because you are loved with an everlasting love. Nothing can change that, but *you* have to accept it.

Acceptance requires the courage to seek the source of this love—God. Owning our evasions and dishonesties, and making a new start through faith in Christ, and the faith *of* Christ—this is what seeking God means. We are emboldened to face our most humiliating problems because we are forgiven in Christ. Then, as we follow him toward self-knowledge, the depth and power of his faith shape our believing. We transcend denial through the courage of spiritual intimacy and the grace of the cross.

Growth toward transformation involves one's spirit, a reaching within and a reaching beyond. Moments of encounter that produce deepened insight, necessary change, and an authentic awareness of the truth promotes this growth.

MEDITATION

Take a moment to clear your head and imagine you are alone in a rowboat on the open sea at night. It is pitch dark. You can see nothing except a faint light beaming from a lighthouse on the shore. You try to row toward the light, but the boat is too encumbered by emergency provisions to traverse the waves. You have no choice but to throw your food, water, clothing, and medical supplies overboard. Having done this, you row ahead, guided by the light, until you reach the safety of shore.

Similarly, excess inner baggage keeps you from moving toward the light of God. These unseen encumbrances are anything that prevents you from loving and worshiping in spirit and truth. Being controlling or perfectionistic, lazy or prejudiced, insecure or judgmental, negative or quick-tempered, proud or hateful—these destructive actions and attitudes maroon your spirit on a turbulent sea blanketed in darkness. Only by acknowledging our sins and shortcomings can we let go of them and progress toward love and light.

Spend some time in self-examination. Look at your life and honestly assess which of your personal qualities are most harmful to yourself and others. What baggage of yours must be thrown overboard so you can move toward the light? Remembering Jesus' words, "The truth will make you free," meditate on where you need to change and grow.

PRAYER

Radiant and righteous God,
the light of your truth shines in my depths;
no darkness can extinguish it.

Because of your love for me,
I can be honest about my shortcomings
without rejecting myself.

Secure in your presence,
no waves of fear discourage me;
no winds of anxiety defeat me.

I continue my journey toward integration,
stronger than all opposition.

For every awakening of truth you have inspired in me,
I give thanks.

These awakenings have loosened the chains of my bondage.

In discovering that your acceptance goes deeper
than my inadequacies and sins and shame,
I have found a mysterious joy.

Yet I confess, O God,
that my dishonesties and evasions stifle this joy,
and I am afraid to let them go.

Complete honesty seems unfamiliar, threatening.

I prefer the comfort of my chains.

(continued)

(continued)

It is easier
to live in denial than to own my inner darkness,
to blame than to accept responsibility,
to wear a mask than to be real.

Help me to change, faithful God.

Confront me with all that is false and inauthentic in me,
that I may cast it out by your power.

Guided by your grace,
my I find the truth that sets me free. Amen.

STEP TO YOUR OWN MUSIC AND YOU'LL NEVER GET LOST

The Challenge of Nonconformity

I have seldom seen such composure. It was Monday, June 5, 1989. The Tiananmen Square massacre had happened the previous day. Wang Weilin, a nineteen-year-old Chinese student, walked into the middle of East Changan Boulevard in Beijing and halted a column of seventeen tanks. Numbed by the terror of the massacre, he must have been at the end of his rope. Yet he acted heroically. Millions watched on television, awed by his courage. He was reportedly sentenced to ten years in prison for his nonviolent intervention.[1]

In those days Jesus came from Nazareth of Galilee and was baptized by John in the Jordan.

MARK 1:9

Wang's decisive action inspires me. The government expected him to accept its rule; the army expected him to cower before its might. He said no. His example illustrates an important truth about the spiritual life: Growth demands nonconformity. People grounded in integrative love heed the voice of conscience; in doing so, their inner calm deepens, even as adversity intensifies.

THE WATER OF WITNESS

The first major event of Jesus' adulthood dramatized his commitment of conscience. When Jesus was about thirty he heard John the Baptist preaching repentance. Those who submitted to John's baptism for the forgiveness of their sins made a statement: They were aligning themselves with his radicalism. John denounced hypocritical religion and corrupt politics; baptism demonstrated solidarity with him. He invited people into the desert, the place of the exodus tradition of transformation. There, far from the rituals of organized religion, they relied only on God, not on their status in the group, for salvation. A new future awaited them, symbolized by the Jordan River, which the Israelites crossed to enter Canaan. Likewise, those baptized by John returned to the Promised Land prepared for the coming kingdom of God.

John's message resonated in Jesus' spirit. In submitting to baptism, Jesus declared his independence from all of society's abusive forces. He died a symbolic death in the Jordan. Becoming as nothing in obedience to God, he was born anew in the Spirit. This rebirth initiated his mission of reordering the world's power structure to respect human dignity. As the Son of God and Son of man, Jesus can make us children of God, like him. A voice from heaven proclaimed his identity, "You are my Son, the Beloved; with you I am well pleased" (Mark 1:11).

To appreciate the significance of Jesus' baptism, remember that he was poor and Jewish. Jews were despised by the Romans in first century Palestine. Jesus grew up oppressed. He knew how military brutality, political ruthlessness, and the divisions of race, class, and sex devastated people.

In Roman society the strong exploited the weak. Raw power reigned on street and battlefield, in court and coliseum. Rulers such as Caesar, Pilate, and Herod exacted exorbitant taxes from those least able to pay: farmers and fishers, craftspeople and peasants. According to the historian Josephus, Jews regarded it as "shameful to continue to pay tax to the Romans and to recognize mortal men as their masters, as well as God."[2] But they had no choice. It was either pay or become slaves, which meant joining perhaps the largest group in the empire.

Legalists branded nonconformists as outcasts, and the outcasts were many. In biblical times, outcasts included blind Bartimaeus, Mary Magdalene, and Zacchaeus the tax collector. Below them were the lepers and beggars, prostitutes and vagrants. These were untouchables as well as outcasts. They lived miserable lives in callous times, abandoned by society, scorned by organized religion.

Jesus believed this was wrong. He expressed his dissent by reaching out to those people who were considered unclean and unacceptable. Jesus attacked this system by insisting that compassion, not holiness, was the essential quality of God and of a life centered in God. Luke quoted him as saying in the Sermon on the Mount: "Be compassionate as God is compassionate" (Luke 6:36). Nothing could have been more radical. Not only did Jesus associate with anyone and everyone, he also healed those considered unclean and made them the heroes of some of his parables. Thus his message was good news to women and the poor, to the diseased and the maimed—to all ostracized or marginalized people.[3]

APART FROM THE CROWD

When guided by an integrative spirituality, we see Jesus' experience as our own. He transcended loyalty to the group and claimed his uniqueness. So must we. If we fail to honor our personhood, we cannot grow, but instead are unconsciously bound by the expectations of others. For instance, we may become perfectionists by trying to meet a parent's impossible standards. Or, if we live in a society where sex and fame are preferred to love, we may accept these distorted values as true.

In Jungian thought, well-being requires that we explore our inner depths and examine our motives, wounds, and insecurities. Having faced the negative consequences of following the crowd, we can choose the way of individuation.

Individuation means discovering not only our uniqueness but also our unity with all life. Self-knowledge fosters self-giving. A whole person disciplines the ego—which is one's view of oneself and the conscious and unconscious feelings that accompany this view—to serve the higher values of the universal human being within. Thus, being an individuated person does not mean being individualistic; it means centering our lives in God, which for Jung is the same as becoming a fully conscious, integrated self. When one seeks this goal, says Jung, "it is as if a river that had run to waste in sluggish side-streams and marshes suddenly found its way back to its proper bed, or as if a stone lying on a germinating seed were lifted away so that the shoot could begin its natural growth."[4]

The journey toward individuation is deeply personal; each of us must find our own way. You know you are on the journey when you heed your inner voice and remain true to yourself. The voice is subtle, but it has been speaking to you all your life. It is firm yet compassionate, honest yet gentle. In your loneliest moments the voice whispers, "You are loved." When you fail, it declares that you're not a failure. The voice calls you beyond yourself. It impels you to keep going when you're exhausted and not to quit when you've been defeated. It invites you to become your most noble, courageous, and loving self. This is the voice of God. It calls you to embrace the highest within you, and to espouse values that are truly your own. You heed the voice of conscience and embrace risk. Ultimately, you gain control of your life and participate in the shaping of your destiny.

I admire a friend of mine who, though a single woman, adopted a child. This woman has wonderful homemaking and nurturing gifts, and she has always wanted to be a mother. She reached her mid-thirties, however, without finding "Mr. Right." Rather than getting depressed about being single, she became proactive in pursuing her dream. It's difficult for a single woman to adopt; many agencies only consider couples. But she refused to quit. She finally found an agency that places "special needs" children. After a long wait and several false starts, she adopted a seven-year-old daughter. Rather than accept the role life cast her in, she rewrote the script.

My favorite nonconformist was my ninety-four-year-old grandmother, who died in June 1994. She and my grandfather immigrated to the United States from the island of Marmara in Turkey more than seventy-five years ago. We called her "Nene," which means "grandmother" in Turkish. Her name, though, was Fotiñie, which means "lady of light." It's a beautiful name with a poetic sound and roots in the Greek-speaking Byzantine empire; that's why she refused to anglicize it or go by "Mrs. Peter Evans, Sr."

Nene took equal pride in her American citizenship and her ethnic heritage. Surrounded by Protestants, she remained fiercely loyal to the Greek Orthodox Church. She sang the "Star-Spangled Banner" as well as Greek dancing songs. She spoke what was on her mind and dressed as she pleased. She bartered for a better price at the supermarket and made no attempt to disguise her heavy accent.

When I was growing up, I wasn't always comfortable with Neñe's uniqueness. But she celebrated it. She attended college at seventy-five, drove a convertible at eighty, starred in a hospital benefit show at eighty-five, and still baked the best Greek food and pastries in Washington State at ninety. She died as independently as she lived. No nursing home for Neñe! She danced to her own music, and invited others to dance with her, until she breathed her last.

IN SEARCH OF INNER TREASURE

Marcus J. Borg also emphasizes Jesus' radical nonconformity. He rejected the purity system of the Jewish culture in which he lived. This system took as its starting point a verse from Leviticus: "You shall be holy, for I the Lord your God am holy" (Lev. 19:2). An elaborate system of rules arose to ensure obedience to this teaching. Life was organized around contrasts between pure and impure, clean and unclean. The result was tremendous suffering for those who failed to meet society's standards.

Jesus invited everyone into his spirituality of consciousness, the kingdom of God. The kingdom "is like treasure hidden in a field, which someone found and hid; then in his joy he goes and sells all that he has and buys that field" (Matt. 13:44). The kingdom is like yeast that leavens bread, or like a mustard seed, which begins small but grows into a great tree. It is like "a merchant in search of fine pearls; on finding one pearl of great value, he went and sold all that he had and bought it" (Matt. 13:45).

To imitate Jesus' faith is to seek this kingdom. It is to celebrate individuality and creativity, not legalism. It requires dying to self and awakening to God. Individuation has a price that few are willing to pay. Those who choose the inward path as Jesus did must "enter through the narrow gate; for the gate is wide and the road is easy that leads to destruction, and there are many who take it. For the gate is narrow and the road is hard that leads to life, and there are few who find it" (Matt: 7:13-14).

I am haunted by the movie *Dead Poets Society.* Each time I watch it, I am challenged by its call to nonconformity. The year is 1959; the scene, Welton Academy, a prestigious boarding school for boys. Mr. John Keating (played by Robin Williams) is the school's new English teacher, unorthodox and passionate. He wants his students to seize each day by being true to themselves. If they do this, he promises, they will make their lives extraordinary.

Mr. Keating's influence inspires some of his teenage students to form a secret club—the Dead Poets Society. Neil Perry (played by Robert Sean Leonard) is their leader. Neil loves acting and has a part in a school play. But his father has other plans. He demands that Neil concentrate all of his energies on becoming a doctor.

As opening night approaches, Neil considers quitting the play to appease his father. Mr. Keating encourages him not to, especially since his father will be out of town that night. Disaster strikes when Neil's father appears at the performance. Neil is brilliant; he receives a standing ovation. But his father is disgusted by the whole affair.

An emotional confrontation occurs later at the Perry home. "We're trying very hard to understand why it is that you insist on defying us," says Mr. Perry, his wife passively at his side. "Whatever the reason, we're not going to let you ruin your life. Tomorrow I'm withdrawing you from Welton and enrolling you in Bratton Military School. You're going to Harvard, and you're going to be a doctor!"

Neil is crushed. After everyone goes to bed, he puts on his acting costume and stares pensively out a window into the winter night. Then he takes out his father's pistol, sits at his father's desk, and pulls the trigger. He chooses to die rather than conform.

Neil's death devastates his friends and creates a crisis at Welton. The headmaster needs a scapegoat. Had it not been for Mr. Keating and the Dead Poets Society, Neil would still be alive, he insists. Mr. Keating is fired. When he returns to his classroom one last time, many of his students honor him. One after another, they stand on their desks and recite one of his favorite lines of poetry, Walt Whitman's' "Oh captain, my captain!" This is their tribute to idealism. In spite of everything, they choose to be as true to themselves as Mr. Keating is to himself. Some students, however, remain seated.

What would you have done? I ask myself that question every time I see the movie. I often imagine myself rising with the other nonconformists to salute Mr. Keating. That is me at my best, a person true to himself. But there's also another me. Like the students who remained seated, I sometimes "go along to get along."

Deep down, we all want to be accepted, to fit in with the crowd. Many times, there's nothing wrong with that. But when we betray our inner values to meet someone else's expectations, we court disaster. Sacrificing our personhood to appease our insecurity, we commit a suicide of character.

Integrative faith shows us a better way. Being baptized into Christ's death and resurrection promises us eternal life, the ultimate security. But this is meant to be a beginning, not an ending. Baptism also reminds us of Jesus' radical individuality and calls us to imitate him. Imitation empowers our spiritual journey; it keeps us seeking the kingdom of God and its treasure of deepened inner awareness. When Jesus' faith becomes our own, we may swim against the tide and risk being disliked. But the risk has a reward—a clear conscience and a growing self-respect.

MEDITATION

Meditate on your baptism. Picture in your mind the water that was used to symbolize your union with the death and resurrection of Christ. Your faith promises you the forgiveness of your sins and new and eternal life in God. Your baptism also commissioned you for ministry in Christ's name.

Use these moments to broaden these meanings. The water is also your conscience. It calls you to keep faith with yourself, to stand against the crowd. Think about Paul's words, "Do not be conformed to this world, but be transformed by the renewing of your minds, so that you may discern what is the will of God—what is good and acceptable and perfect" (Rom. 12:2). Honestly admit the ways in which you are still a conformist; let God's healing presence show you where you need to change. Envision yourself bravely following Christ, stepping to the beat of a different drummer, even in the face of persecution.

PRAYER

O God of the inner voice and upward call,
who urges me to forsake convenience
and embrace conscience,
hear my prayer.

I come not expecting miracles
but seeking strength.

Life is both beautiful and terrible;
it inspires and overwhelms me.

That's why I need you, dear God, to see me through,
and you never fail me.

When I rejoice,
you share my celebration.

When I weep,
your heart breaks along with mine.

I thank you for your unfailing presence.

But I want more of you, Lord.

Not in earthquakes, wind, or fire,
but in whispers of grace do I find you.

Sometimes I feel alone.

To escape my isolation,
I follow the crowd.

(continued)

(continued)

Fitting in consoles me;
I need to be part of the group,
for you created me to love and be loved.

I am not ashamed of my need for relationships,
but I confess how easily I compromise my
values in order to be accepted.

Keep me truer to myself, O God.

May I not "go along to get along"
but seek first your kingdom.

Remind me of Jesus in the Jordan;
let me go with him there in my spirit every day.

Rekindle in me the meaning of my baptism,
that I might be cleansed afresh by its water
and challenged anew by its witness. Amen.

DISCIPLINE YOUR DESIRE AND FIND INNER POWER

The Challenge of Freedom

My wife and I met in a seminary library. A friend had given Carol some well-intentioned advice: "Don't allow yourself the luxury of falling in love." Knowing that she wanted to pursue doctoral studies, he was saying, "Keep your heart free. Don't get attached; you might get hurt. Then your goal will be doubly hard to achieve."

I wish someone had given *me* that advice. While Carol refrained from romantic attachments, I fell in love—with her. She got "A"s; I got "B"s, even a couple of "C"s. I paid dearly for my lack of inner discipline. Emotional involvement without spiritual boundaries makes one vulnerable to pain. When Carol didn't return my affection, I got depressed. It wasn't the first time. It had happened in previous relationships when my desire for a woman's love went unfulfilled. With Carol I was fortunate. She changed her mind, and we fell in love and got married. Still, I bear wounds from sacrificing my centeredness on the altar of attachment.

Chances are, you have wounds, too. You have known the pain of wanting something you could not have. Your desire for this illusive something permeated your thoughts and consumed your energies. But rather than try to discipline your desire, you surrendered to it, and it took control of your life. You imprisoned yourself in a cell of your own making.

Jesus, full of the Holy Spirit, refturned from the Jordan and was led by the Spirit in the wilderness, where for forty days he was tempted by the devil.

LUKE 4:1–2

God created us not for this bondage but for freedom. Freedom is the gift of the integrative love that nurtured the inner life of Jesus. We are free when we trust that everything we need for contentment is within us. This trust enables us to treasure the sacredness of the present moment. We stop clinging to desire and start letting go. Rather than cursing our frustrations and bemoaning our grief, we give them to God. Our burdens lightened, we feel grateful and offer praise. This is freedom: to celebrate life in the faith of Jesus Christ. But finding this freedom requires that we understand unnecessary attachment and learn how it can be overcome.

THE GREATEST TEMPTATION OF ALL

The word *attachment,* notes psychiatrist Gerald G. May, derives from an Old French word meaning "nailed to." We taste anguish when attachment deflects our innate desire for God and "nails" it instead to specific people or processes, objects or substances, thereby creating addiction. "Addiction also makes idolaters of us all," says May, "because it forces us to worship these objects of attachment, thereby preventing us from truly, freely loving God and one another." [1]

You know you are attached when you become obsessed. It often happens subtly. Say you enjoy your work. The more time and energy you devote to it the more promotions and raises you receive. You feel affirmed, so you make sacrifices to increase your success. Soon you have no identity apart from your job. You become a workaholic.

Or maybe you want an attractive body. You eat right, exercise daily, and keep yourself well groomed. But there's a cost—guilt. You can't splurge on a dessert or miss a workout without hating yourself. What's worse is finding a new wrinkle or, God forbid, getting gray hair. These experiences depress you. Fixated on having a perfect body, you're miserable.

Some of us become attached to material things, so we "shop 'til we drop." Others can't get through the weekend without a "fix" of professional sports. Still others are addicted to alcohol or drugs, ideas or relationships, gambling or sex, power or money.

No one escapes attachment's allure. Not even Jesus avoided it completely. The story of his temptation in the wilderness contains guidance for keeping us free. To deepen his spirituality after baptism, he spent forty days in desolation, fasting and praying. Such intensive solitude was necessary before he began his ministry. Without deepened inner awareness he could be deterred from his mission to the cross. The success of his ministry depended on the quality of his integration. Before beginning to preach, he sought to unite his conscious with his unconscious, his body with his spirit, his faith with his deepest motives.

But contemplation promises no paradise. One may encounter terror in the inner world. God can be found there, but evil may lurk there, too. Penetrating the unconscious in introspection means, in Jung's words, "the outbreak of intense spiritual suffering; it is as when a flourishing civilization is abandoned to invading hordes of barbarians, or when fertile fields are exposed by the bursting of a dam to a raging torrent."[2]

Looking within can be traumatic because it brings one in contact with what Jung called the *shadow*. The shadow is the dark side of human nature. It resides in the unconscious, containing our potential for evil, our unacceptable impulses, shameful desires, and haunting inferiorities. We often repress the shadow. Because it contradicts the way we want to see ourselves and have others see us, we try to deny its existence. But repression does not rob the shadow of its power. It surfaces in the form of compulsions and projections that undermine intimacy and create both inner turmoil and social upheaval. This is why Jung believed that wholeness begins with acknowledging the shadow's presence within. Integrating the shadow into one's conscious sense of self actually advances the individuation process. In fact, such integration unleashes the potential of the soul for transformation and discovery.

When brought into the light of consciousness, said Jung, the shadow is "ninety percent pure gold." Being aware of our destructive traits and dispositions gives us power over them; struggling with them builds strength and character. Increasing our awareness may even enable us to put these traits and dispositions to constructive use. For instance, if you recognize aggression as part of your shadow, you can discipline your tendency toward violence. At the same time, you can retrieve from your aggression the good quality of assertiveness, much needed in a competitive world.

It takes a high degree of self-knowledge to discover the shadow's gold; most people never make this discovery. As a result, not only do they fail to achieve their full potential, but they also fall victim to their darkest urges and the unhappiness sown by those urges.

The devil personifies this sinister side of the shadow in the story of Jesus' temptation in the desert. The Greek word *diaballo,* from which comes "devil" in English, literally means "to throw something across one's path."[3] The devil bargained for Jesus' soul, making narcissism and idolatry look glamorous instead of toxic. He threw these stumbling blocks across Jesus' path, hoping he will fall into attachment. This would destroy him.

THE PERILS OF THE WILDERNESS

The Adversary first tempts Jesus to "command this stone to become a loaf of bread" (Luke 4:3). Attachment to materialism beckons in his words. The devil hopes that Jesus will sacrifice his freedom by abusing his divine power, by placing the physical above the spiritual.

Jesus knows that while the poor want food for the body, they also need food for the soul. The more bread they have, observes psychological commentator Fritz Kunkel, the less they will "enter the painful struggle toward spiritual evolution, for which we need dissatisfaction."[4]

Having all of our material needs met leads to the addiction of wanting more. We become preoccupied with acquiring the latest gadgets and goodies, and never look within. Materialism originates in inner emptiness. To paraphrase St. John Chrysostom, poverty has less to do with what we have than with what we want.

We cannot be free while yearning for more. The object of our desire takes on the quality of bread: We must have it to live. Thus we sacrifice all to satisfy our material cravings, but we feel disillusioned when the sacrifices intensify rather than heal our alienation.

An episode of "The Twilight Zone" television series of the 1960s describes our predicament. A man dies violently. Having not lived an exemplary life, he is surprised to wake up to an experience that seems idyllic. He can't miss a pool shot. Women succumb to him. Anything he wants, he gets. He thinks he's in heaven. But as his every wish is fulfilled, a sense of horror overtakes him. He realizes he's not in heaven, but in hell.

Hell is where the devil wants Jesus to go. He tries to get him attached to a material object—bread—and the process of creating it from stone.

But Jesus sees through the devil's scheme. The deepest hunger is spiritual, not physical. External comforts cannot produce internal transformation. Jesus remains free by proclaiming a biblical truth: "One does not live by bread alone" (Luke 4:4).

Next, the devil offers Jesus all the kingdoms of the world if he will worship him. Ever the cunning manipulator, the evil one believes, as did the English clergyman Charles Caleb Colton, that "power will intoxicate the best hearts, as wine the strongest heads." The Jews' yearning for deliverance from Roman oppression underlies Satan's ploy. They wanted a conquering king, not a suffering servant, as their Messiah. He tempts Jesus to grant their wish. He promises him the world—for a price. All Jesus has to do is honor the devil as God.

To rule the world is the narcissist's dream. The person in charge enjoys the spoils of power: security, pleasure, the adulation of the masses. Who could ask for more? No one, taught the German philosopher Friedrich Nietzsche. He believed that the primary human drive is the "will to power," as did Alfred Adler, one of the founders of modern psychology. This is the original deadly attachment—the desire to be God.

Power, said Henry Kissinger, is the ultimate aphrodisiac. The quest for it, whether in the home or workplace, government or church, seduces many people, like Goethe's Faust, to sell their souls to the devil.

Addicted to power and its rewards, we make bad choices. We exchange freedom for status and control. The price is regret. Jesus took a different approach. He stood his ground and asserted his boundaries, refusing to participate in the devil's idolatry. Jesus' kingdom is not about conquest but about integrative love. His answer emphasizes this: "Worship the Lord your God, and serve only him" (Luke 4:8).

The third temptation builds on the other two. The devil places Jesus on the pinnacle of the Temple in Jerusalem and dares him to throw himself down. This is the temptation to test God.

If Jesus accepted the dare, he would limit God by coercing him to honor human demands above divine intentions.

This is the devil's fiercest attempt to lure Jesus into dependency. A seductive message resonates in his dare: "Come on, Jesus, have a little fun. Leave the wilderness behind. Experience a thrill. Attachment is as invigorating as a leap into thin air." Many of us believe this lie and end up forfeiting our centeredness to appease someone else's craziness. Unmet spiritual needs motivate this self-destructive behavior. We get hurt because our sense of self is grounded in our performance and not in our intrinsic value.

Desperate to prove ourselves worthy of our own inner affirmation, we use people rather than love them. This creates what Jewish theologian Martin Buber calls an "I-It" relationship, in which the "I" manipulates another person as an object—the "It." Manipulators operate with an inflated sense of self-importance that dehumanizes the other person in a relationship. This prevents both of them from achieving an "I-Thou" relationship, in which each honors the other's personhood. The result is an "It-It" relationship. When one person treats another as an "it," both become "its." But both are elevated to the status of "thou" when they treat each other with mutual respect, thereby forming the basis for a "Thou-Thou" relationship.[5] Sustained by God's word, Jesus refused to accept less from Satan. He resisted the temptations of attachment and experienced freedom. The devil had no choice but to flee.

INCOMPLETENESS AND POSSIBILITY

I am both encouraged and rebuked by Jesus' example. He demonstrates that attachment can be resisted; freedom lies in imitating him. But his triumph in the wilderness also confronts me with my weakness. His centeredness went deep enough to sustain him; mine is often too shallow to do the same for me.

We become attached because we fear emptiness. Our fear keeps us yearning for fulfillment. We flee the wilderness within in pursuit of the perfect career, marriage, or lifestyle, not realizing that our quest is motivated by a lack of spiritual depth. Then we are disappointed when no success is gratifying enough, no love intimate enough, no pleasure ecstatic enough to satisfy us.

Jesus could not be manipulated by the devil because his consciousness was perfectly attuned to God's will. His inner development was so advanced that he saw the temptations as the lies they were. Having come to terms with his shadow, he knew his weaknesses. Such self-knowledge is the beginning of freedom because it empowers one to choose good over evil. The shadow must be restrained so it does not lure the soul to indulge its darker passions. Restraining the shadow through spiritual discipline gives one not only moral equilibrium, but also the satisfaction of having faced temptation and conquered it.

Jesus practiced this discipline and bore the fruit of its rewards. Having accepted inner dissonance as part of the individuation process, he steered into his vulnerabilities, not away from them, during forty days of testing. Finally his shadow fled. This shows that, as Thomas à Kempis remarked, "We must each wage a long and fierce inner struggle before we learn to master ourselves fully and to focus all of our love on God."[6]

The inner struggle is a clash between our potential and our fear. We naturally embrace the good in ourselves and shun the evil. But to disown our shadow is to stymie our personal development. We must face what we fear in order to resolve our inner incongruities and release the psychic energy of integration. By befriending our shadow, we can retrieve its gold and channel our desire in positive directions.

By embracing life's unfinished essence and loving the unfinished parts of ourselves, our incompleteness inspires our creativity and kindles our passion. The yearning in our heart is there for a reason. God placed the yearning there to woo us into the divine embrace. "Our hearts are restless," prayed Augustine, "until they rest in Thee."

Our restlessness is a gift that can lead us to our heart's true home, provided that our desire for the things of this world becomes a greater desire for the things of God. Of all classical Christian writers, John of the Cross offers the most vivid description of this reorientation. He contends that spiritual intimacy involves filling our emptiness with God. We must "cast out strange Gods, all alien affections and attachments."[7] This is done in the "dark night of the soul," the ultimate place of purification. Through this period of desolation, the will is stripped of all its cravings, and the soul quickened by a deepened knowledge of God.

John likens this "state of union" to the relationship between a burning piece of wood and the fire that engulfs it. Just as the wood is eventually transformed into flame, so the surrendered soul is made one with God; it has "no other function than that of an altar on which God is adored in praise and love."[8]

Combining faith *in* Jesus with the faith *of* Jesus helps us persevere through the "dark night" of our wilderness experiences. Sometimes this perseverance can only be understood by relying on psychotherapy, spiritual direction, or a support group. Through this reliance, integrative spirituality becomes more than a theory, it becomes a life-giving discipline.

Temptation cannot prevail. As Jesus emerged from the wilderness with a deepened self-understanding and passion for God, so can we. The secret is in heeding his words, "But strive first for the kingdom of God and his righteousness, and all these things will be given to you as well" (Matt. 6:33).

MEDITATION

Use the image suggested by John of the Cross in your spiritual practice. Your relationship with God is like the relationship between a burning piece of wood and the flame that engulfs it. Total combustion symbolizes mystical union, the goal of the spiritual life.

Meditate on the flame of a candle or, in your mind, envision God as fire. Your attachments are like wood that refuses to be consumed; they prevent you from becoming one with the flame and its promise of illumination and freedom. As each attachment surfaces, explore what unmet spiritual need underlies it.

Surrender these needs to God. Ask for help in accepting the barrenness of not having them met. Become aware of how idolatry can arise from the wilderness within. Explore ways in which grace can sustain you, and find inspiration in the biblical sayings Jesus used to resist temptation. You may want to focus your meditation by repeating a phrase such as, "May your love alone kindle the flame of my desire, O God."

PRAYER

From the bondage of addiction
to the freedom of faith,
I flee to you, O God.

I come acknowledging my enslaved desire;
I need deliverance.

Rather than wanting you above all things,
I let other gods seduce me.

I am attached to people and possessions,
ideas and agendas,
activities and rewards.

The problem is my emptiness: I try to fill it
from the outside rather than from within.

In the wilderness of unfulfilled yearning,
I easily succumb to temptation.

Only in your presence, gracious God,
do I find the strength to resist.

You give me courage to face my barrenness.

Because you love me,
I can stop running.

Rather than fleeing into
unhealthy relationships and destructive behaviors,
I can rest in you.

Take me deeper into your rest,
I pray.

When I am tempted by attachment,
remind me of the cost of giving in.

May I seek fulfillment not in fleeting satisfactions
but in lasting faith.

Direct my passion toward you
and away from false gods.

Fill my emptiness with your presence,
until my heart becomes an altar
and your love the flame.

Then I will know you fully,
even as I am fully known,
and in this knowledge,
I will rejoice. Amen.

YOU'LL NEVER WALK ALONE IF YOU HAVE LOVE WITHIN

The Challenge of Friendship

"I've never felt so alone!" The words of an older friend of mine cut to my heart. He was describing dining out by himself after losing his wife. In his eighties, he braved the restaurant scene in search of togetherness, but found isolation instead. "It was terrible," he said. "The restaurant was full of people, but no one spoke to me. They talked and laughed and enjoyed their meals as if I were invisible. All I could think of was how much I missed my wife and how out of place I felt. Being with people was supposed to help me with my grief. Instead, it made the grief worse. I went home and wept."

I felt like weeping with him. Though I have never lost a spouse, I, too, have known loneliness. It battered my heart as a boy whenever my family moved, which was often. It accompanied me to college, where I worked nights as a desk clerk in a deserted and dingy YMCA lobby. When I attended a seminary 3,000 miles from home, I felt the loneliness of separation from my family. Now Sunday afternoons are hard. I love being with my congregation for worship and fellowship, but soon everyone goes home, and the empty church assaults my spirit with loneliness.

> *The next day John again was standing with two of his disciples, and as he watched Jesus walk by, he exclaimed, "Look, here is the Lamb of God!" The two disciples heard him say this, and they followed Jesus.*
>
> JOHN 1:35–37

It is likely that you have had similar experiences. Perhaps you feel lonely when the days grow short and the weather turns cold in the fall. Maybe loneliness assails you during the holidays. Perhaps you are bearing heavy burdens and have no one to share them with. Loneliness may have smitten you amid failure, defeat, or betrayal, and pierced your heart when you lost a close relationship.

"All religion, all life, all art, all expression come down to this," said the American journalist and playwright Don Marquis: "to the effort of the human soul to break through its barrier of loneliness, of intolerable loneliness, and make some contact with another seeking soul, or with what all souls seek, which is (by any name) God."[1] This is the human predicament. Alone we are born; alone we die. In between, we yearn for intimacy and mutuality, for the delights of knowing and being known in love. So strong and persistent is this yearning that it shapes our identities.

A SPIRITUALITY OF TOGETHERNESS

Jesus knew this yearning, too. As he continued his journey of individuation, he sought followers among whom to embody integrative love. From this embodiment arises true friendship, the antidote for loneliness. After encountering God in his baptism and wilderness, Jesus wanted others to have similar experiences. Love cannot exist in a vacuum; it must be expressed in relationships. Thus, Jesus committed himself to a cluster of friends and journeyed with them toward spiritual discovery.

Jesus brought harmony to the fragmented pieces of the disciples' lives. They found a new beginning in friendship with him, each other, and their inner selves. This becomes evident in John's account of the calling of four of the disciples.

Each of the four had some personality flaw. Since Andrew's name is so closely associated with Simon Peter, his extroverted brother, one wonders whether Andrew had sufficiently developed his own individuality. Peter, on the other hand, may have been too extroverted: He often spoke and acted without thinking. On one occasion he publicly scorned the idea of Jesus going to the cross; on another, he drew his sword and cut off Malchus's ear in Gethsemane. After professing a willingness to die with Jesus, Peter denied him instead.

Philip was a disciple intolerant of ambiguity. At the Last Supper, Philip demanded that Jesus reveal God to him. Earlier, Philip became frustrated in a crowd of five thousand hungry people. He saw no way they could be fed and doubted whether Jesus knew a way either.

Philip's friend Nathanael also appears in John's narrative. Nathanael's struggle with negativity is evident in his remark about Jesus' hometown of Nazareth. A mocking, cynical tone can be detected in his words, "Can anything good come out of Nazareth?"

It was no easy task for Jesus to befriend these disintegrated personalities and forge them into a community of caring. To do this he had to model integrative love for them. They grew in character and commitment, forgiveness and faith, in response to his example. Granted, love's lessons didn't always stick, as in the tragic case of Judas. Yet Jesus poured out his life practicing among the twelve what he preached to the multitudes.

He offered them abundant life in the agape that was the source of his own centeredness. The Quaker mystic Rufus Jones contends that the Greek word *agape* should never have been translated as "love" in English. "Love," with its overtones of romantic sentimentality, is neither deep nor comprehensive enough to communicate the full meaning of *agape*. Instead, *agape* should have remained untranslated, the name for the new principle that Christ proclaimed. Agape is "the divine perpendicular confrontation," the spontaneous, unconditional, all-embracing love of God in the free gift of Christ's pardoning grace.[2]

Once kindled in your heart, agape produces self-esteem and confidence. It enables you to claim your uniqueness and find power within. What can defeat you if the most powerful force in the universe is on your side? Agape helps you to develop your sense of self-worth so that you relate to others out of strength, not weakness. You form meaningful friendships because you have overcome your inner alienation. By befriending the God who befriends you in Christ, you celebrate the gift of integrative love.

As Jesus and his disciples bonded in friendship, they learned to accept one another just as they were. Caring friends communicate this acceptance in concrete ways. They listen without interrupting, empathize without pitying, confront without condemning, and support without patronizing. Agape makes friendship possible by casting out fear. It creates the mutual trust and vulnerability that heal loneliness.

A Hasidic story tells of a man who got lost while walking through a forest. He took one path after another to try to find his way back to town, but each led him astray and he wandered in circles for hours. He was overjoyed when he met another traveler. He said to him, "Thank God for another human being. Can you show me the way back to town?" "No," said the other man, "I'm lost too. But I know how we can help each other. I will tell you which paths I have tried and been disappointed in, and you can do the same for me. Working together, we'll find the one path that leads out."

Without caring friends, we get lost in the forest of isolation. We wander in circles seeking the warmth we crave. Power and wealth, impersonal sex and macho success, obsessive thoughts and addictive behaviors. Our relationships inward, outward, and Godward become the growing edge of our spiritual becoming, leading from isolation to integration. These relationships bring out the best in us by helping us bring out the best in others.

INTIMACY'S ENEMY

According to the psychology of individuation, a dark foe sabotages our pursuit of interpersonal communion. That foe is our self-absorbed ego. As the sum total of what we know (or think we know) about ourselves, the ego is the center of our conscious life; it is the part of our personality that we project to the world. When the ego turns inward, it obstructs growth. Such preoccupation with self is what depth psychologists call egocentricity and the Bible calls sin. The egocentric ego, says therapist Fritz Kunkel, is the devil. It so corrupts a person's spirituality that it creates hell within.

But this need not happen. The ego can spur individuation when vitally connected to the real self, the soul's deepest ground, the image of God at the core of the personality. This core, or center, is the source of love and creativity. When rooted in the center, the ego responds to life in a way "exactly appropriate to the kind of situation with which a person is faced," says Kunkel. "It cannot be stylized or characterized because the creative ego response is always unique and one-of-a-kind." Conversely, a dysfunctional ego response evokes "inflexibility, panic, defensiveness, rage, and sterility."[3]

Psychotherapy teaches people to be true to their center. It seeks to establish and then to strengthen what has been called the ego-self axis. Put in Christian terms, the goal of the inner quest is to banish sin by imitating Christ and maximizing the image of God in oneself. Whether understood psychologically or spiritually, becoming complete means surrendering to love. Kunkel contends that love cannot be feigned or willed; it must come from the heart if it is to be genuine. Love abides in the center. As the center shines through the personality, it inspires loving relationships. But these relationships cannot form as long as the ego remains egocentric and blocks the flow of love from within.[4]

Through friendship with his closest followers, Jesus demonstrated how to live beyond egocentricity. Many were the ways he showed his love for them: saving them from a storm at sea, healing Peter's mother-in-law, raising Mary and Martha's brother Lazarus from the dead, washing the disciples' feet, giving his life on the cross. He called them to imitation when he said, "Take my yoke upon you, and learn from me" (Matt. 11:29). But their egocentricity prevented them from obeying.

James and John wanted to "command fire to come down from heaven" to destroy a Samaritan village that would not receive Jesus (Luke 9:52-54). On another occasion they requested prominent places in heaven, one at Jesus' right hand, the other at his left. But he rebuked their presumptuousness and reminded them that "whoever wishes to become great among you must be your servant, and whoever wishes to be first among you must be slave of all" (Mark 10:43-44). Peter's denials of the Lord and Judas's betrayal are further examples of the disciples' egocentricity.

The disciples' actions seem so incriminating because we see ourselves in them. We experience the same insecurity that motivated their excesses. Transcending egocentricity requires becoming conscious by listening to our depths. This is what Jesus did—he maintained an inner connection with his center. His experience of integrative love empowered him to be a friend. Friends were essential to his spirituality. He sparred with them in conversation, listened to their concerns, forgave them when they hurt him, celebrated their joys, and shared their sorrows.

When with them, he was tough enough to be tender and secure enough to be vulnerable.

We cannot become all we are meant to be on our own. Imitating Christ means bonding with others. His pattern of mutuality has far-reaching implications. Husbands and wives, parents and children, teachers and students, employers and employees—all make the most of their relationships when they practice mutual respect.

THE HUMAN FACE OF GRACE

Egocentricity deadens; friendship enlivens. Friendship is life's most enriching experience. Jesus succeeded at it because of his profound inner harmony. He remained centered in God in all of his relationships. Centered people offer their friends the right blend of intimacy and space. Because they are reconciled to their own emptiness, they do not expect other people to fill it. They love with no strings attached and remain free of relationship addictions. Their presence is a gift of grace.

A friend of the respected religious educator Parker Palmer embodied this gift. Palmer was deeply depressed. Various people tried to bring light into his darkness with well-intentioned encouragement and advice. Nothing worked. But this friend took a different approach. He came to Palmer's home every afternoon at around four o'clock, sat him in a chair, removed his shoes, and massaged his feet. He hardly said a word, but his healing presence restored Palmer's hope.

Such compassion enriches life and promotes transformation. When we love from our center, we have friends because centeredness is attractive; it rings of authenticity, breaks down barriers, and invites a positive response. Every friendship has its own spirituality. Ideally we become like Christ, giving love as we have received it from God. When this happens, we conquer our egocentricity and touch each other's depths.

When you share your heart with me, you welcome me into your inner world. I hear my own hopes and fears expressed in yours. By letting down your defenses, you pay me a compliment: you trust me. Trust makes the communion of our spirits possible. It frees us to share our feelings with each other—our agony and ecstasy, our perplexity and peace. In this sharing we touch life's wonder as well as its tragedy. Awakened to love's presence, we bond in friendship.

Jesus' words to his disciples on the night of his betrayal convey the joy he experienced through friendship. The setting was the upper room in which he and his disciples shared their final meal. Having washed their feet, he gave them a new commandment: he mandated that we love one another as he has loved us—in mutual self-giving. Indeed, "no one has greater love than this, to lay down one's life for one's friends" (John 15:13). The reward of this integrative loving is that, in his words, "my joy may be in you, and your joy may be complete" (John 15:11). Those who imitate his love receive his highest compliment: "I do not call you servants any longer, because the servant does not know what the master is doing; but I have called you friends" (John 15:15).

MEDITATION

Be present to God in solitude. In the stillness remember friends who have touched your life. Welcome them into your heart as you meditate. Recall times of laughter and tears, adventure and discovery, sharing and caring. Savor the memories. Experience again the warmth and acceptance and togetherness you felt. Perhaps some of these people live far from you; others may have died. Yet they are part of you, and you are part of them. Thank God for each person. Love came to you through them; they are gifts to your soul.

Meditate on how your friends have helped you encounter God. Celebrate the spiritual qualities in them that you admire, and ask God to cultivate these qualities in you. Affirm that your friends are more important to you than wealth or possessions, success or status. Remind yourself that you are only as isolated as you choose to be. You have much to give others if you would seize the opportunity to do so. Begin by asking, How can I be a better friend? Reach into your center and find integration as you express love inward, outward, and Godward.

PRAYER

Befriending God,
who in Jesus Christ invites me into intimacy,
I come to you longing to love and be loved.

I wait for you in silence.

Your voice speaks in my depths,
calling me by name.

You knew me before the world began,
and you know me now.

Even when others exclude me,
ignore me,
reject me,
you receive me as your own child,
precious in your sight,
secure in your embrace.

I thank you.

Because of your love,
I can be alone without being lonely.

I do not bemoan my isolation
but celebrate the solitude of this moment.

You are always seeking me,
assuring me of your presence.

(continued)

(continued)

When I am centered in your acceptance,
I am free to love without dependency or addiction.

Help me to share this love in true friendship,
I pray.

Deliver me from the self-centeredness that alienates me
from you and others and myself.

May I not only bring your presence to my relationships
but find it in them as well. Amen.

WANTING WHAT YOU HAVE BEATS HAVING WHAT YOU WANT

The Challenge of Contentment

eing centered in integrative love enables us to find contentment. Discontent arises when we want what we do not have. Trying to attain the unattainable produces drive. Our spiritual journeys stall in the quicksands of obsessive-compulsive behavior that not only cripples our efficiency but also makes us frustrated, embittered people.

I find the hope of deliverance in the attitude of a certain Maine fisherman. He lay by a river lazily casting his line into the water. Supplied with a six-pack of beer and a homemade lunch, he caught enough salmon to keep him interested but not overworked. A businessman from town approached him and asked, "Don't you realize that you could catch more fish if you put several lines into the water at the same time?"

"Why would I want more fish?" asked the fisherman.

"If you had more fish," said the businessman, "you could sell them at a profit. Then you could buy a big fishing boat with the money. In time you could open a store and sell your fish to the whole town. After you opened one store, you could expand to a second and third. Eventually you could start a wholesale fish

When Jesus saw the crowds, he went up the mountain; and after he sat down, his disciples came to him. Then he began to speak and taught them . . .

MATTHEW 5:1–2

business, employ hundreds of people, and ship fish all over America. You could get rich!"

Taking a swig of beer, the fisherman looked unconvinced. "And then what would I do?" he asked

"Why, then you'd have all the time in the world. You could relax and go fishing!"

Smiling, the fisherman replied, "Well, what do you think I'm doing now?"[1]

Contentment is a matter of perspective. It involves savoring the moment. It comes from listening to your intuition and honoring your inner values. Contented people do not chase fantasies, nor do they magnify their problems. They know themselves and like who they are, make the best of their circumstances, and reverence life's goodness.

Although favorable external conditions may foster contentment, they do not guarantee it. You can be wealthy and famous, powerful and sexy, but still lack peace. I am haunted by this paradox. Some people feel empty though they have so much. Others live joyfully although they have very little. Why? Because those who listen to their depths gain access to the spiritual wisdom that exists at the heart of life. This wisdom exists beneath the turmoil of external events. Living from the depths yields the self-knowledge that nurtures contentment.

But many people are alienated from their inner selves. Because their souls are anchored to shallow moorings, they seek fulfillment in external stimuli rather than from within, and they never find it. Instead they become their own worst enemies. "When one unconsciously works against oneself," wrote Jung, "the result is impatience, irritability, and an impotent longing to get one's opponent down whatever the means."[2] Simply put, discontent arises from unexamined living.

THE CALL TO CREATIVITY

In the Sermon on the Mount, Jesus proclaims a better way. Fritz Kunkle calls this Sermon "The Magna Carta of Spiritual Evolution."[3] It teaches that contentment comes not from indulging one's passions but from mastering them through creative discipline.

Creativity spawns inner growth. It gives birth to a new consciousness. It is possible to transcend one's fears and faults, compulsions and prejudices, by exploring their root causes. The Sermon on the Mount invites us to undertake this exploration. It unlocks the door to Jesus' inner life and welcomes us in. A verse in the middle of the sermon provides insight into the whole: "Be perfect, therefore, as your heavenly Father is perfect" (Matthew 5:48).

"Perfect" here should not be misinterpreted as meaning "perfectionism," that is, never making a mistake. Jesus' understanding of perfection was rooted in the Greek concept of *telos*, which means "end" or "goal." As the One who embraces the beginning and end of all things, God is perfect in this sense. God lacks nothing and exists eternally in love as creation's Source and Goal.

To be perfect, as God is perfect, is to fulfill one's purpose. It is to become whole and complete in love, as God is whole and complete in love. Christ was perfect in this way; imitating him enhances our spiritual development. Living in harmony with our inner essence and the essence of life, as Jesus did, is the secret of contentment. But the secret gets lost when people revere the letter of God's law rather than the spirit of the law.

Legalism thwarts creativity. The Sermon on the Mount celebrates the law's deeper meaning—the call to love God, others, and self as a unity. Divorce and murder, stealing and coveting, slander and adultery—these problems can be avoided by practicing this integrative love. Love turns the other cheek, goes the extra mile, and embraces enemies as well as friends. When we become whole and complete in love, we fulfill our highest destiny. We stop our anxious striving and rest in God. In touch with our depths, we find contentment. In the words of the English poet Robert Southwell, "Not where I breathe, but where I love, I live."

A RUT TO AVOID

Perfectionists fantasize compulsively about how life could be better. They miss the joy of "good enough" by coveting better and best. They are never satisfied with themselves, their circumstances, or their performance. Nor can others hope to meet their standards. "A perfectionist," states an anonymous aphorism, "is someone who takes great pains—and gives them to someone else."

In northern Canada, where frigid temperatures leave huge potholes in the roads, a sign along a highway reads, "Take care which rut you choose; you will be in it for the next 25 miles." Perfectionism is a rut that destroys contentment. It stems from the shadow, which Jung called "one's own unknown face." As the discordant dimension of the personal unconscious, the shadow is the disowned feelings, volatile passions, and submerged evil within.

If not recognized and integrated into one's consciousness, the shadow will manifest itself in projections. Life will be seen through the lens of the shadow's distortions and dishonesties. Perfectionism is a form of projection. It leads us to expect more from circumstances, relationships, and people than they can give. Thus, we become preoccupied with "a world whose reality remains forever unattainable," as Jung said. [4]

While our minds know that this unattainable world is an illusion, our hearts are seduced by it. Contentment vanishes. Rather than accepting the mediocre within and around us, we try to eliminate it. Attempting the impossible, we lose our sanity.

Jesus dealt creatively with this problem. He loved people in spite of their flaws. He had special affection for those considered imperfect by society—the tax collectors, prostitutes, lepers, and beggars. He also forgave people's moral imperfections, as in the case of the woman taken in adultery, the thief on the cross, and Peter, who denied him.

Imperfections can be blessings in disguise. They push us to our limits and force us to be resourceful. They challenge us to use our intelligence, imagination, and ingenuity to find solutions. Responding to imperfection, we encounter grace. Without life's flaws, we would not grow; boredom would overwhelm us.

John A. Sanford notes that inner growth results from confronting the imperfections in ourselves. Our lust and greed and selfishness make the law necessary. But, contrary to what the scribes and Pharisees thought, the law is not the highest form of morality. Following the law restrains destructive actions but does not change the toxic attitudes that cause them. The higher morality, says Sanford, "requires confronting the shadowy one within us who has made the rules necessary in the first place." [5]

Our "shadowy one" feeds on discontent. Whatever we wish were different about our lives becomes a potential source of attachment and suffering. Most desires, once fulfilled, are replaced by new ones. We can get trapped by always wanting more. This discontent fuels the drivenness that makes each day a grind. Worse, it churns up the destructive passions that Jesus condemns in the Sermon on the Mount, all of which stem from alienation within. The answer lies not in fulfilling all of our desires, which is impossible, but in learning to be content in spite of life's imperfections. As author and radio personality Garrison Keillor says, "Some luck lies in not getting what you thought you wanted but getting what you have, which once you have it you may be smart enough to see is what you would have wanted had you known." [6]

TOWARD DEEPER SURRENDER

Contentment is a discipline. You begin to learn it by asking, What prevents me from being whole here and now? In other words, What must I surrender before I can be free? Your answer to these questions will become the challenge of your inner work. Self-knowledge underlies the contentment that is the reward of rising to this challenge.

Although we don't doubt the importance of knowing ourselves better, we struggle with what is required to do so. I understand intellectually that in order to deepen in self-knowledge I must examine my past wounds. I know I must explore what lies beneath my insecurity. I must confront the sources of the depression that sometimes assaults me. Such introspection makes me face my weaknesses and sins. It can appear threatening—but, seen in terms of the spirituality of Jesus, is not a threat but an invitation. When I model my inner life on his, I am invited into the same consciousness of God's will that he had. To the extent that I align my attitudes and actions with this divine will, I find contentment even amid struggle.

Fritz Kunkel believes that this evolution of consciousness is the goal of both psychology and religion. The Sermon on the Mount illuminates this goal, advocating total surrender as the way toward integration in one's inner life. The sermon is now more relevant than ever. The materialistic and self-centered values of North American culture have created a spiritual crisis. The problems that Jesus decried in the sermon still flourish in contemporary society. Stories of violence, sexual exploitation, and relational dysfunction dominate the evening news. How can this be changed? The Sermon on the Mount suggests that the change must come from within.

The psychology of individuation corroborates this view. According to Jung, "Individuation is the life in God."[7] Egocentricity stifles this life. It makes an idol of self and constricts spiritual growth. Selfish people cannot love. They are too preoccupied with meeting their own needs to give of themselves to others. Jung advocates inner discipline as the path toward growth: "For this, certain virtues like attention, conscientiousness, patience, etc., are of great value."[8]

The imitation of Christ fosters individuation because Christ models virtue for us. The ideals of the Sermon on the Mount were fulfilled in his life: He was tempted "in every respect. . . as we are, yet without sin" (Heb. 4:15). As theologian Gabriel Fackre explains, we are not talking about "a pedantic tabulation of the perfect record of a moral and spiritual virtuoso. . . . Rather, the sinlessness of Jesus is the capacity of this figure in its firmness of intent and constancy of character to direct the eye of faith to the Vision of God."[9]

Admiral Richard E. Byrd, the famous explorer, nearly died in Antarctica during the winter of 1934. Venturing out into the fog and cold, he pounded a stick into the ice every thirty yards or so to leave a trail to find his way back.

But Byrd walked beyond his sticks and got lost. He built a mound, about eighteen inches high, out of ice and snow. The mound became his center. Fixing his eyes on two stars on the horizon, he walked out 100 paces, looked for his sticks, and, not finding them, returned to the mound. Then he repeated this process several times in other directions. If he didn't find his sticks, he always returned to the mound at the center of his radius. At last, on one of his jaunts out from his mound, he sighted his sticks and followed them home.[10]

Contentment is found by returning to center, as Byrd did. Our center is God, the One in whom we find refuge when feeling discontent. The center never moves. It resides in life's depths, accessible to seeking hearts. This means we are never completely lost. Inner fragmentation may disorient us, but by returning to center, we can find integration. The spirituality of Jesus invites us home and inspires the courage that discipline requires. Hearing and heeding its call offers the hope of self-transcendence. And no one is more content than those who live in this hope.

MEDITATION

Close your eyes and imagine you are standing beside an old well. You are hot and thirsty. In order to get water from the well, you must lower the bucket. But the rope is too short. It will only lengthen as you expel unhealthy yearnings from your inner life, allowing you to dip your bucket in the deep water of contentment and drink from it. Be attentive to your breathing. Each time you inhale, pray the words, "I need you, O God." Each time you exhale, name some destructive desire from which you wish to be freed. Here are some examples:

I need you, O God; I don't need wealth.

I need you, O God; I don't need power.

I need you, O God; I don't need success.

I need you, O God; I don't need youth.

I need you, O God; I don't need sexual ecstasy.

I need you, O God; I don't need a perfect job.

I need you, O God; I don't need a perfect marriage.

I need you, O God; I don't need perfect children.

With each cycle of inhaling and exhaling, imagine the rope lengthening. When you have rid yourself of perfectionistic longings, your bucket will reach the water of contentment, which is the water of God. Drink and be satisfied.

PRAYER

Giving and forgiving God,
in you I find everything I need.

You provide day and night,
sunshine and rain,
food and shelter,
grace and peace.

Why do I look elsewhere for contentment?

Abundant life begins and ends with you.

Without you I could gain the whole world
and still be poor.

My material blessings come from your hand.

So do my cherished relationships and
my inner awareness of your presence.

I thank you for all you have given me
and for what you have made me.

My problem is that I want perfection;
I am intolerant of flaws.

Rather than celebrate the good I have,
I bemoan the best I lack.

Reveal to me my ingratitude
and failure to love.

(continued)

(continued)

*Help me embrace the disowned parts of myself
that I might be easier on others
and find peace within.*

Purge perfectionism from my heart.

*Remind me that to find contentment
I must rest in you;
I must accept what I cannot change
and allow myself
to be molded in positive ways
by negative experiences.*

*Only by surrendering to you
does this molding begin.*

*May I surrender anew here and now,
and may I find contentent in you
this day and always. Amen.*

7

IF YOU SETTLE FOR HAPPINESS, YOU'LL MISS THE BEST

The Challenge of Wholeness

One of my favorite stories of New England is about a tourist driving near Boston who got lost and needed directions. Coming upon a young boy working in a field, he asked, "Son, how far is it to Boston?"

The boy answered, "If you keep going the way you're headed, it's about a 25,000 miles. but if you turn around and go the other way, you'll find Boston sixteen miles down this very road."

I identify with the tourist. Tired of inner turmoil, I seek integration, but I often get lost in pursuit of it. Tough relationships lead me off course; anxiety and insecurities blind my vision, and emotional distress bogs me down. The American ideal of happiness is a particularly seductive

When he entered Capernaum, a centurion came to him, appearing to him and saying, "Lord, my servant is lying at home paralyzed, in terrible distress." And he said to him, "I will come and cure him."

MATTHEW 8:5-7

detour. When I take it, integration eludes me, and I travel 25,000 miles in the wrong direction.

You probably know this ideal well. You see it dramatized on television, hear it extolled on the radio, and encounter it in best-selling books, hit movies, and "feel-good" religion. The ideal implies that doing more and having more are better than being more. Happiness is an emotional high found in rewards and possessions outside yourself. To be happy is to be the master of your fate, the captain of your soul.

But we Americans, on the whole, are not happy people, nor do we live in a happy society. Life in the fast lane has caused moral confusion. Cutthroat competition has spawned an epidemic of stress and loneliness. Rampant materialism has produced spiritual bankruptcy. Violence reigns. We have not learned that, in the words of psychologist David G. Myers, "Happiness is less a matter of getting what we want than wanting what we have."[1] Commercially exploited and environmentally endangered, politically cynical and artistically stagnant, sexually obsessed and psychologically anxious—how ironic to find ourselves in this condition after all these years of pursuing happiness!

IN THE STEPS OF THE GREAT PHYSICIAN

The imitation of Christ leads us beyond happiness to wholeness. Although these two qualities share some characteristics, they differ in important ways. Whereas happiness depends on optimal external conditions, wholeness is an internal state of being. Happiness is a fleeting emotion; wholeness, a resilient spiritual presence.

Anyone with a satisfying career, fulfilling relationships, and freedom from major trauma can be happy; wholeness requires integrative love. Christ shows us the way. His faith connected him to love in his inner depths. Yet imitating him offers no quick fixes, no easy answers, but healing insights. Imitation calls us to love amid all the emptiness and fullness, grief and joy, pain and promise we find in our depths.

We often fail. Love requires too much honesty and courage—too much pain—for us to answer its call. We often shun Jesus' faith and take detours of 25,000 miles in search of inner stability. Only by aiming for wholeness will we avoid this mistake and find integration.

That Jesus aimed for wholeness can be seen in his role as healer, which is emphasized in all four Gospels. To imitate Jesus is to share the pain of others. Compassion is essential to individuation; in becoming healers we are ourselves healed. The Gospels record forty-one distinct accounts of Jesus' therapeutic interventions, dramatic examples of an extensive ministry.

Except for miracles in general, this is by far the greatest emphasis given to any one kind of experience.[2]

The eighth chapter of Matthew, for instance, records several healings. Jesus' compassion toward a Roman centurion's servant reveals much about his continuing journey of individuation. The Romans and the Jews hated each other. The Jews regarded the Romans as military oppressors, while the Romans scorned the Jews for being separatists who refused to worship the emperor. Jesus transcended this conflict. A Roman centurion's servant lay paralyzed. The centurion, who commanded one hundred men in the army, came to Jesus in despair. Rather than sending him away, Jesus offered to come and cure the servant. The centurion's concern for a man whom many considered to be property evoked Jesus' empathy. He proclaimed the universality of his kingdom in response to the centurion's humility and faith: Gentiles as well as Jews will share the messianic banquet in heaven. "Go," said Jesus to the centurion, "let it be done for you according to your faith" (Matt. 8:13). The servant was healed in that hour.

FINDING PROMISE IN PAIN

Examine this incident and see Jesus' radical love. He tolerated no stereotypes, pandered to no prejudices, sympathized with no animosities. He saw humanity as one. His treatment of the centurion broke down barriers of religion, race, and culture; his healing of the servant showed his solidarity with the poor. From the depths of his humanity and the heights of his divinity he offered wholeness to both men—a centurion with a broken heart, a servant with a broken body.

Jesus made this offer from his center. His centeredness manifested itself in his extraordinary personal integration of extroversion and introversion, thinking and feeling, masculinity and femininity. John A. Sanford contends that from a Jungian perspective Jesus was whole.[3] Although his human vulnerability led him through emptiness and doubt to perplexity and brokenness, he found hope amid struggle because of his intimacy with God.

Jesus was what author Henri J. M. Nouwen calls a "wounded healer"; his compassion arose from his own inner tensions and pain. So must ours. Wholeness is not ecstatic bliss but quiet trust. Being whole does not mean never being sad or depressed, lonely or confused; Jesus experienced these feelings. Being whole does not mean always being strong, always feeling good about ourselves. Nor does it mean being free from problems. You become whole by loving in spite of your wounds. Your wounds are a sign of life, an incubator of creativity; they force you to rely on grace. Granted, you may resent having been hurt, and if you could relive the past, you might change many things. But without the hurt, you would not have discovered your inner strength. You also would not have touched the depths of your humanity.

Your wounds make you feel. Hidden in your pain is the capacity for you. While you believe that life's joy is more than its pain, the pain has taught you much. Its greatest lesson is that your suffering bonds you to other sufferers and increases your compassion. Even when not appreciated, compassion triumphs, for it manifests grace, the active expression of God's love.

Although grace may not end our discontent or melancholy, it sustains us amid these conditions. It redeems our brokenness and infuses thanksgiving into faint and doubting hearts. Grace is God meeting us in our need and embracing us in wholeness. To be a wounded healer is to share grace with another and journey toward wholeness together. Failing to realize this, we become obsessed with our own wounds and increase our misery.

A couple I knew, Barry and Marianne, married in their early twenties. Because they were both working on graduate degrees, they postponed having children. After they had finished school, various financial pressures kept them from trying to start a family until Marianne was thirty-five. But after trying for five years, they still hadn't conceived. Despite their material blessings, they were grieving their infertility. Each of them blamed the other for their barrenness. They were trapped in separate worlds of sadness, and the root of their pain was their lost opportunity to have children.

Like many modern couples, Barry and Marianne may have postponed their family because they were absorbed by their financial and career goals. Their grief runs deep; it always will. But all is not lost. Hope for healing lies in binding the wounds of others, perhaps by adopting a child, becoming foster parents, or helping other infertile couples adjust to their situation.

Unfortunately, the American dream of "life, liberty, and the pursuit of happiness" does not promote such giving and helping.

The dream promotes individualism, not individuation. To be happy is to have your conflicts resolved, questions answered, hurts healed, and desires fulfilled—or so the dream implies. Jung recognized the folly of such naiveté when he wrote that "individualism means . . . giving prominence to some supposed peculiarity rather than to collective considerations and obligations. But individuation means precisely the better and more complete fulfillment of the collective qualities of the human being."[4] Self-absorption cannot produce fulfillment; it alienates people from collective qualities such as mercy and charity.

A FAITH WITH A HEART

We need a spirituality that connects us with our own inner selves and the selves of others. The fulfillment we seek lies in a unity of consciousness and unconsciousness, body and soul, individuality and community. The English word *salvation* derives from the Latin *salvare,* which means "to make whole." Integrating faith *in* Jesus with the faith *of* Jesus saves our sanity by making us whole in compassion. As wounded healers, we still suffer—but not alone. Our pain is lessened because it is shared.

Christianity celebrates caring. The inseparability of faith and compassion in Jesus' message and ministry distinguishes him among world religious leaders. He practiced spiritual discipline not to gain success or fulfillment, not to escape life's tumult, but to do God's will by embodying integrative love. He was too disturbed by social injustice, religious hypocrisy, and his disciples' inconsistencies to have peace of mind. Yet he was whole—wounded, but whole. Sharing the pain of hurting people helped him bear his own pain.

Fritz Kunkel's "We Psychology" describes the kind of wholeness Jesus knew. Kunkel believes that fulfilling one's true self cannot be done in isolation; it requires depth relationships with others. These relationships move a person from egocentricity to creativity. In order for this movement to occur, two or more individuals are necessary, because only in community does the self, which is not "I" but "We," emerge.[5] "To find oneself," says Kunkel, "means at the same time finding the We—and to find the We is to find oneself."[6]

Wholeness is a corporate matter. I cannot be all that I am meant to be until you are all that you are meant to be. Jesus' compassion toward the centurion and his servant demonstrated this. It was compassion rooted in justice and inclusiveness. As such, it expressed God's yearning for the healing of society and each individual. To act compassionately is to participate in this yearning and to share in God's wholeness.

Naomi Remen, a physician who uses art and meditation in the healing of cancer patients, tells of a twenty-four-year-old amputee who became depressed when he lost a leg at the hip to bone cancer. When Dr. Remen asked him to draw a picture of his life, he sketched a vase with a deep crack running through it. It took intensive inner work for him to rebuild his self-image.

Developing compassion for other amputees, whom he began visiting in the hospital, helped him to heal. On one occasion, he encountered a young singer who was so bitter about the loss of her breasts that she refused to look at him. As the radio played over the hospital intercom, he took a risk. Removing his prosthesis, he began dancing around the room on one leg, snapping his fingers to the music. She looked up, amazed. Then she burst out laughing and said, "Man, if you can dance, I can sing."

Some time later, Dr. Remen showed the man the picture of the cracked vase he had drawn. His response was, "This isn't finished yet." He took a yellow crayon, colored over the crack, and said, "You see, here—where it is broken—this is where the light comes through."[7] He learned that our hearts grow strong at the broken places when we become wounded healers.[7] We forget our own wounds as we concentrate on healing others.

Some people are obsessed with their pain. It engulfs them. They wallow in it. The pain becomes their source of meaning and identity; they would be lost without it. They need to let go of self-pity and embrace empathy. Sharing the brokenness of another might be the first step toward healing for them both.

Jesus' healing of the centurion's servant was only one of many such miracles. Lepers and tax collectors, prostitutes and beggars—these he also restored to health. He saw himself not as separate from them but as one of them. Those who would imitate Christ, writes Henri Nouwen, see their own brokenness and pain "not as sources of despair and bitterness, but as signs that they have to travel on in obedience to the calling sounds of their own wounds."[8]

I once counseled a woman who claimed to be a victim of satanic ritual abuse. Her story of childhood torture is the most horrific I have heard as a pastor. She was a broken person who had carved the words "I hate myself" into her arm with a razor blade, and she had attempted suicide several times. She only improved when she became an advocate for other victims of ritual abuse and began leading support groups for them. Glimpsing wholeness through the lens of her own compassion, she struggled toward it with faltering steps.

Her story reminds me that healing is seldom simple. Nor is it ever complete in this life, especially if your problems are long-standing and complex. Imitating Christ won't end your loneliness or confusion, your boredom or alienation. But it is a place to begin. Though you will never be fully whole here and now, you can know moments of wholeness and integrative love. Being a pastor reminds me of this daily. I feel God's presence when praying with people in the hospital, comforting them at funerals, counseling them in times of crisis, or working with them in social ministry. When my heart touches the heart of another, I am embraced by the heart of God. In this embrace, I find peace and affirm the words of Mother Teresa of Calcutta, "We can do no great things; only small things with great love." The love we give, whether great or small, returns to us as wholeness. When we are whole, we will never fall into despair.

MEDITATION

Find a quiet place and take a few moments to enter into a reflective mood. Seat yourself in a reverent position and close your eyes. Celebrate your union with God in Christ. You and your Creator are no longer strangers; you are part of each other, bonded in love.

Savor this gift in your spirit and use the acronym "LUFA" to remember the phrase, "I am Loved, Understood, Forgiven, and Accepted in Jesus Christ."* Move deep inside yourself. Let your most intimate concerns enter your consciousness. You may be concerned about your mistakes, failures, health, sexuality, appearance, intelligence, marriage, friendships, addictions, inadequacies, fears, losses, or insecurities. As you contemplate each of these, breath deeply and affirm, "I am Loved, Understood, Forgiven, and Accepted in Jesus Christ." God's presence will help you cope. Receive this presence by applying the LUFA phrase to whatever turmoil you feel. Surrender to wholeness and grow in integration.

*This idea originated with Leslie D. Weatherhead, pastor of City Temple in London during World War II.

PRATER

Into your presence I come, inviting God,
not because I must, but because I may.

My soul thirsts for you.

I am empty unless filled with your Spirit,
anxious unless clamed by your peace,
lost unless guided by your word.

Receive me once more, O welcoming Savior.

Cast me not away from your presence,
though I understand little of your ways.

I want easy answers;
you prefer that I live the questions.

I crave fulfillment;
you call me to faith.

I expect immediate results;
you teach me to wait.

Grant me a deeper perspective, O Lord.

May I see my inner opposites not as annoying
    inconveniences
but as catalysts of growth.

(continued)

(continued)

Remind me that true integration
is not freedom from struggle,
but life in your presence.

Let me not settle for less.

Deliver me from the perils of leisure without labor,
pleasure without accountability,
happiness without character.

Instead, awaken your kingdom within me—
the kingdom beyond race or class,
age or sex,
language or nation—
that as an instrument of your peace,
I might find peace in my heart.

May wholeness be my goal,
not only for myself but for the world,
and may love be my guide. Amen.

YOU CAN BE IN THE STORM WITHOUT LETTING THE STORM BE IN YOU

The Challenge of Adventure

Have you heard of Nahshon ben Aminadov? Let me tell you about him. The authors of the Midrash claimed that Nahshon ben Aminadov inspired God. According to them, his courage saved the Israelites at the Red Sea. They were trapped. Drowning awaited them if they went forward; enslavement by the Egyptians if they retreated.

But God parted the waters. The Midrash authors explained this miracle by lauding the heroism of the head of the tribe of Judah, Nahshon ben Aminadov. Only after he dove head-first into the Red Sea did God roll back the waters. Then the people walked across on dry ground.[1]

He woke up and rebuked the wind, and said to the sea, "Peace! Be still!" Then the wind ceased, and there was a dead calm. He said to them, "Why are you afraid? Have you no faith?"

MARK 4:39–40

Though fictional, this story illustrates an important truth. There are places on our spiritual journeys where danger lurks ahead and behind us. Like the Israelites, we feel trapped, unable to return to the past or advance into the future. Under such circumstances, Nahshon ben Aminadov's example provides guidance: The only way out is through. Growth requires heroism, the willingness to live or die by one's risks. The call to integration is the call to adventure. Nahshon ben Aminadov heard this call and dove into the water rather than stagnate on dry ground. Life summons us to do the same, and the summons often comes amid crisis.

A FAITH FOR THE STORM

Depth psychology emphasizes the role of the unconscious in illuminating the way through our problems. We must ask ourselves, What deeper wounds and unresolved issues lie beneath our melancholy or anger, our guilt or depression? Only as we see our problems as challenges and our life as an adventure will we grow toward integration. Jung calls this the hero's journey. Virtually all cultures have hero myths; the myth resides in the human psyche. Jung saw the hero as "a self-representation of the longing of the unconscious, of its unquenched and unquenchable desire for the light of consciousness." [2]

To know is to understand. We seek knowledge of ourselves and others, of life and God. But attaining this knowledge is painful; it requires an encounter with the inner self. The person who has this encounter, wrote Jung, "passes from joy to sorrow, from sorrow to joy, and, like the sun, now stands high at the zenith and now is plunged into darkest night, only to rise again in new splendor." [3]

Jung's concept of the hero incorporates a spirituality of adventure. Maintaining our integrity and self-awareness amid struggle demands a questing spirit. Jesus shows the way. That he fits the hero paradigm becomes evident as he crosses the Sea of Galilee with his disciples. A terrifying storm arises. The wind and waves batter the boat, nearly swamping it. All the while Jesus sleeps in the stern, undisturbed. The disciples panic. Fearing for their lives, they wake him and demand, "Teacher, do you not care that we are perishing?" (Mark 4:38). He responds by rebuking the wind and the waves. The storm ends. In the ensuing calm, he asks, "Why are you afraid? Have you still no faith?" (Mark 4:40).

Fritz Kunkel emphasizes the inner meaning of this experience. A storm at sea, like a storm in a dream, is an age-old symbol of the "perils of the soul" during a time of crisis. Mythologists call this passage through crisis "the Night-Sea Journey." It promotes the hero's inner development. [4] Jesus is strengthened within by maintaining his poise under pressure.

But notice his role with the disciples. He takes them along on the adventure, then leaves them alone to face a storm. Yet he does not desert them; he is only sleeping, ready to help if needed. They must imitate him by relying on their faith to sustain them. They fail. Rather than remaining centered in God, they succumb to fear. This reveals their lack of individuation. In response, Jesus loses patience and expresses disappointment at their spiritual immaturity.

THE IMPERATIVE OF INNER WORK

We come from God, live in and through God, and return to God. The journey in between requires attentiveness. Detachment from one's depths stymies growth; insight inward promotes centeredness. This becomes evident in the contrasting reactions of Jesus and the disciples during the storm. He saw the storm as a test of faith; they saw it as a catastrophe. These differing reactions arose from different states of consciousness. Jesus was connected to his center; the disciples were alienated from theirs. In his center Jesus found peace and power and thus remained calm. Just as his awareness of God's presence emboldened him, so the disciples' lack of awareness defeated them.

This story asks, Who are we most like? The point of the story is that those who imitate him stay grounded in their center and find calm amid life's storms.

I think of two people who endured crises, but with different results. Tony founded a self-help organization to give juvenile offenders a second chance. The courts referred them to him after their release from prison. Relying on corporate sponsors, his organization helped these troubled young people find jobs. The program thrived. But soon the long hours, media recognition, and power struggles within the organization took their toll on Tony.

He had a nervous breakdown. When I visited him in the hospital, he said to me, "Evan, I'm afraid to die, but I'm more afraid to live." He had invested so much in his work that his world crumbled when things went wrong. Nominally religious, he had no spiritual resources to sustain him; he felt abandoned by God. After several attempts to take his life, he finally succeeded with a drug overdose. I think of him often and miss him. His story reminds me of the peril of emphasizing external rewards more than inner integration.

Susanne also experienced a crisis. She dreamed of becoming a professor of English. Having earned outstanding grades in college, she enrolled in a Ph.D. program at a respected midwestern university. After six years of sweat and sacrifice, she passed her qualifying exams and began her dissertation. Then trouble struck. Her professors were either too uninterested or too busy to read her material. Moreover, they competed rather than cooperated with each other, and she got caught in the crossfire. After two years of frustration, she quit. She saved her marriage and her sanity, but she cannot teach without her doctorate.

Such a major disappointment would devastate many people, but not Susanne. Though she had to settle for a clerical job, she shuns bitterness. Her faith is her rock. She refuses to interpret her experience as a failure. God was with her in her despair, and she discovered her inner strength. She learned that new dreams can be born when old dreams die. Her family became more important than her career; her friends more precious than a Ph.D. She sees her loss as an ending, but also as a beginning. One door had to close so that others could open within her and around her. Such is the adventure of faith. It calls us to find God amid crisis.

This is the hero's journey. As Jesus took the journey on the Sea of Galilee, so must we take it each day. It is a journey inward. We are invited, says mythologist Joseph Campbell, "into depths where obscure resistances are overcome, and long lost, forgotten powers are revivified, to be made available for the transfiguration of the world." A life lived from the depths "becomes penetrated by an all-suffusing, all-sustaining love, and a knowledge of its own unconquered power." [5]

Many of us probably prefer fast relief for our turmoil, but none exists. Lasting solutions emerge from painful inner work. Many people remember their dreams more regularly during a crisis. Reflecting on our dreams connects us to our unconscious, enabling us to explore the symbolic meanings hidden there. From this exploration can emerge new insights into your life and circumstances. But retrieving these insights may require painful self-confrontation. The pain signifies new life within us, longing to be born. We can curse our fate, yearn for rescue, yell at God, but unless we listen to our depths, we cannot be transformed.

Listening empowers. Becoming conscious of our insecurities is the first step to overcoming them. Healing our wounds and dependencies begins with acknowledging them. The goal is integration, and it cannot be achieved without supplementing faith *in* Jesus with the faith *of* Jesus.

FINDING GRACE IN TRUST

When we seek God in our turmoil, we practice a spirituality of adventure. We learn that crisis is not the opposite of centeredness but an element in centeredness. The crisis makes us go deeper into God, the source of calm at the eye of the storm. In the depths we encounter grace, the only quality sufficient to sustain us.

Grace is at the heart of life. The sunset and the dawn bear witness to it. Grace reverberates in the wind whistling through the trees. It can be felt in a warm embrace, seen in a flower's beauty, tasted in a hot meal on a cold day. Oh, to live in grace! To smell coffee brewing in the morning, watch the snow fall, hear a symphony, go to work, make friends, fall in love, laugh and cry, compete and learn—such are the gifts of grace.

But trouble comes in spite of them. Sometimes we must tolerate the intolerable and accept the unacceptable. Peace is found by remaining centered. Centeredness is part skill, part gift, part commitment. Grace for the daily grind emerges from it. A life centered in God becomes not painless but adventurous. Being grounded in God's acceptance emboldens one to take the risks necessary for growth. This means living by faith, not panicking as the disciples did on the Sea of Galilee.

To trust is to remain centered in integrative love when crisis strikes. Love is a decision, not just an emotion. Faithfulness to its call can be excruciatingly painful, but its long-term reward is the realization of the self. People who love find that God comes through in the pinch. It may take time; darkness may descend, and questions, doubts, and fears assail. But eventually God gives hope that enables the heroic response that the problems and crises in our life demand.

As Carol S. Pearson writes in *The Hero Within,* "Every time we confront death-in-life we confront a dragon, and every time we choose life over nonlife and move deeper into the ongoing discovery of who we are, we vanquish the dragon."[6] Discovering who we are means becoming conscious. It means uncovering the illusions we have of ourselves so that we might be transformed by truth and meaning. Life's storms make this journey necessary. Taking it builds character.

There once was a man who dropped out of grade school, ran a country store, and went broke. Fifteen years passed before he paid his bills. He got married but never made his wife happy. He was defeated twice while running for Congress and twice more while campaigning for the Senate. He delivered a fine speech to an indifferent audience, and half his country despised him. Yet countless numbers of people have been inspired by this awkward-looking man who signed his name, "A. Lincoln."

Greatness is a matter of weathering storms. Weathering storms requires faith. Faith motivates action; it is for participants. The way of faith is the way of adventure. It keeps us involved and seeking. It challenges our fears and stimulates our growth. We need to remember this when darkness descends on our spirits. Crises instruct, and battles with inner demons can increase one's will to win. Failures may come, dreams die, tragedies strike, but all mature the soul.

God is not only in the Big Picture but also in the details. If that's true, the pieces of our lives somehow fit together. The spiritual quest is about finding the pattern and weaving the pieces into it. On this adventure of faith, ordinary people become heroes. When they cannot go ahead or back, they find a way through—like Nahshon ben Aminadov—and their heroism inspires even God.

MEDITATION

Bring the storms of your life to God in silence. Your storms are the struggles, problems, or crises that weigh heavily on your mind and heart. They may involve your relationships or your finances, your work or your health, your addictions or your sexuality, your moral choices or a host of other concerns. It is tempting to panic in the midst of these. Your first response may be to curse the storm, to resent having to deal with it. But no amount of cursing or resentment will make it go away.

As you come to God with the storm raging within you, ask for the grace to see it as an important passage on your spiritual journey. Meditate on what can be learned from it, on how you can see the storm as an adventure rather than a trial. Allow yourself to feel the storm's unfairness and to grieve. But also try to see how it might be a blessing in disguise. When you feel God's presence, you will find the calm at the eye of the storm. Finding this eye is the challenge of your inner work. Persevere in your meditation, believing that calm can be found if you wait long enough and listen attentively enough.

PRAYER

I come to you in this sacred moment,
O God of every time and every place.

Each day reminds me of my need for you.

I need you in my doubt to restore my faith.
I need you in my emptiness to fill the void.
I need you in my turmoil to center me in peace.

You do not disappoint me.

When clouds gather on the horizons of my soul,
your Spirit gives me courage.

I seek this courage now.

Many storms are brewing within and around me;
they cause me to fear.

I am more like the disciples than like Jesus:
I panic.

Life's sea is so great,
and my boat is so small.

If only I could remember
that my problems call me to adventure.

You go with me into every situation.

Even when my bad choices
land me on the rocky shoals of brokenness,
you do not desert me.

Your love never fails.

Remind me that good
can come out of the worst circumstances.

Teach me the lessons I need to learn from my struggles,
that I might grow in character and hope.

Deliver me from the illusion
that this growth comes easily.

By accepting pain as inevitable,
may I render suffering optional,
and may I be in the storm
without letting the storm be in me. Amen.

LETTING GO OF WHAT YOU CAN'T CHANGE SAVES YOUR SANITY

The Challenge of Acceptance

T hink for a moment about the worst crises of your life. Relive the fear and pain they evoked. Then ask yourself, What inner attitude was most responsible for bringing you to the end of your rope? Answering this question myself, I realized it was my failure to practice acceptance. Sometimes I curse life's unfairness until my anger becomes depression. Other times, I try to correct the unfairness on my own power and wind up exhausted. This is because I often lack the serenity, as the Alcoholics Anonymous prayer says, "to accept the things I cannot change, the courage to change the things I can, and the wisdom to know the difference."

He said, "Abba, Father, for you all things are possible; remove this cup from me; yet, not what I want, but what you want."

MARK 14:36

Acceptance is a spiritual skill. Mastering it takes a lifetime. As a teenager, I broke the femur bone in my left leg during a backyard football game. This injury changed my life. Not only did I spend two months in a full body cast, but I also ended up with my left leg shorter than my right. When the doctor told me I must give up sports indefinitely, I was devastated.

Grief set in. I felt angry and demoralized. It took me a long time to find a new identity. Rather than playing on the basketball team (my passion at the time), I became team manager and felt humiliated at having to hand out towels and keep statistics instead of scoring baskets. Only grace, in the form of friends and music and reading, saved my sanity. Moving with my family to the island of Guam was also a great experience. Because the level of competition was lower there, I was able to play basketball again. Through these experiences and the passing of time, grace brought me to acceptance.

The older I get, the more I realize that grieving our losses is life's deepest hurt, a hurt that throbs in all of us at some level every day. Life forces us to let go of one thing after another: our youthful appearance, our physical vitality, and some of our dreams. These are but a few of what author Judith Viorst calls "necessary losses."[1] Because they are as innumerable as they are unavoidable, they magnify our need for grace. Only by grace can we resolve our grief and experience rebirth through acceptance.

The most powerful expression of grace comes to us through the cross of the cosmic Christ, who takes away the sin of the world. But we also encounter grace in the spirituality of the man Jesus. Imitating his reliance on grace teaches us the discipline of acceptance and centers us in God.

SEEKING LIGHT IN DARKNESS

Jesus' experience in the Garden of Gethsemane demonstrates his centeredness. After sharing the Last Supper with his disciples, he went to the garden to pray. Peter and James and John went with him. He knew something momentous was about to happen. Darkness descended on his spirit. Leaving the disciples, he prayed alone, "grieved, even to death." Suffering awaited him, and he knew it. The question was, Would he accept God's will?

Time stood still as he agonized over his destiny. Throwing himself to the ground, he prayed, "Abba, Father, for you all things are possible; remove this cup from me; yet, not what I want, but what you want" (Mark 14:36). These honest words, spoken from the heart, express surrender. They bristle with pain yet celebrate acceptance. Jesus placed his future in God's hands, saying to himself, "I don't know what will happen next; I only know that God will take care of me."

His mindfulness was so complete that he let go of his own desires and embraced God's intentions. In prayer he transcended the image of God as a distant and demanding law-giver.

Instead, he knew God as a loving parent in whose presence he felt secure. Having integrated divine love into his depths, he acted from what Fritz Kunkel calls "the higher consciousness," the inner intuition that all things blend together into "infinite growth." "If we love God," says Kunkel, "we love our fate, and we love the creative event [which takes place within us]."[2] Experiencing this love rooted Jesus in an unshakable centeredness. It not only enabled him to face the unknown alone but also empowered him to forgive his betrayer, Judas, who carried his shadow. In Kunkel's words, "Only by accepting and loving his own Shadow could Jesus redeem the Shadow of mankind."[3]

Carl Jung marveled at the integration Jesus demonstrated. Although under no illusions about how hard it would be "to live one's own life as truly as Christ lived his," Jung felt that the "imitation of Christ" could spur a person toward individuation.[4] Facing adverse circumstances and events is critical to this process. Growth occurs when adversity forces us to draw on our untapped inner resources. When Jung observed this growth in his patients, he noted that "the new thing came to them out of obscure possibilities either outside or inside themselves; they accepted it and developed further by means of it."[5] These people, said Jung , "came to themselves, they could accept themselves, they were able to become reconciled to themselves, and thus were reconciled to adverse circumstances and events. This is almost like what used to be expressed by saying, "He has made his peace with God."[6] Such acceptance transforms lives, bringing freedom from the inner alienation that breeds brokenness.

As these statements show, inner turmoil stems from wanting to change things you cannot change. When we live in acceptance, our turmoil ceases. It is natural to lament the injustice of our adversities; to wish things had been different. But when we go to extremes to try to change things, we give those things power over us and divert our attention from worthwhile pursuits; our creativity gets stymied and we become broken persons.

SEEKING PEACE IN SILENCE

The simple act of acceptance changes everything. A power shift occurs in your heart. You let go of your need to be in control. Rather than obsessing about what you cannot change, you put yourself in God's hands, as Jesus did in the garden. Entering the quietness within, you find peace. But getting to this place is one of the ongoing challenges of the spiritual life. Some losses or wounds take years to accept. The process is fluid. Having reached acceptance at one time, you may lose it again and need to seek it at a deeper level later.

In surrendering to God's will in the garden, Jesus found power within and committed himself to the way of love, even if it meant accepting the cross. To imitate him, says Thomas à Kempis, is to pray: "Lord, you know what is best. Let this or that be done as you wish. Give what you want, how much you want and when you want. Do with me as you think best and as best pleases you and in a way which will give you greater honor." [7]

Contemplative prayer makes us aware of what we need to accept. Images of people and events that hurt us surface as we stop talking and listen. We remember sins, feel passions, confront fears, admit loneliness, celebrate joys. God speaks in the silence and says, "Whatever you are feeling, turn it over to me. Receive my grace for your guilt. Exchange your confusion for my wisdom. Rest in my love. Let my presence be your peace. In me you will find all you need."

Our minds often wander in meditation. The paths they travel may uncover something crying for acceptance. Beneath thoughts of past rejections, failures, or losses may lie pain that went ungrieved. Beneath lustful thoughts may lie estrangement in a committed relationship or loneliness. Beneath thoughts of wealth and fame may lie insecurity. We avoid these deeper issues out of fear. But failing to face what needs to be accepted, we remain in bondage to inner turmoil. Overcoming this bondage requires the confidence that we are strong enough to face anything, with God's help. The sooner the source of the pain is accepted the sooner it will pass.

There was once a powerful king who became depressed. After many days the depression did not end. With the stability of his country at risk, the king called in his sages. He told them, "I need your help. You must find me a special ring, one that will calm my anxiety and restore my joy when I am sad."

The wise men consulted with each other and threw themselves into deep thought. Finally they reached a decision about the kind of ring that would please their king. They devised a ring for him on which were inscribed the words, "THIS, TOO, SHALL PASS."

Remembering those words, we can grieve our losses through to acceptance. This takes time and a faith that trusts in grace. You can't expect healing to happen overnight. Enduring the pain is part of the process. If you listen to your depression, it will guide your inner work. Explore what lies beneath your despair. Is there something you want but cannot have? Has something been taken from you that you can never regain? Only by surrendering these losses to God and journeying toward acceptance will you find peace.

Integrative love nurtures this peace. Knowing that you are accepted unconditionally by God empowers you to accept yourself and others in imitation of Christ. The deeper your integration goes, the more you let go of what you would like to change but can't. Your depression lifts. In the freedom of acceptance, life begins anew.

SEEKING BEAUTY IN BROKENNESS

Unfortunately, some Christians never experience this newness. Their spirituality, based on flawed expectations, won't let them. Perhaps they have heard a preacher promise that Jesus will make their dreams come true. Or maybe they see Christianity as a simple set of "spiritual laws," or a step-by-step formula for salvation and success. What happens when they find themselves in Gethsemane? Chances are, they become disillusioned. Told that all would be well if they accepted Jesus as their Savior, they feel betrayed and defeated by adversity. This is because they see problems, doubts, and fears as enemies of faith, not as elements within faith.

I had a rude awakening as a pastor. It came when I realized that people can espouse flawless theology without becoming whole. Some find it easier to affirm doctrines than to give their hearts to God in an intimate relationship. Granted, doctrinal correctness has its place. But if it produces rigidity in faith, doctrine can stymie rather than stimulate spiritual growth.

Rigidity attempts to look externally strong because it is internally weak. It arises from fear, not love, and hides doubts behind forced smiles and biblical proof texts. Rigidity shares the approach of a Methodist minister who wrote in the margin of his sermon, "Weak point. Pound pulpit harder!"

People estranged from love try to work their way to God. They justify their compulsivity by calling it dedication. Because uncertainty threatens them, they take refuge in cut-and-dried answers to complex questions. Their faith is an exact science, more like math than art.

An integrative spirituality banishes the fear that permeates this mindset. Combining faith *in* Jesus with the faith *of* Jesus fosters centeredness by emphasizing both belief and practice. In Gethsemane he allowed himself to be lonely and afraid, anxious and uncertain. He accepted the ambiguity of not knowing what the next day would bring. Some scholars even think he questioned whether he was the Messiah. Yet he did not quit. He remained true to himself and to God, grounded in a faith deeper than his questions.

This faith heals because it affirms the human condition in its fullness. Life's goal is not to understand but to trust. In trusting we come to understand—and to accept. As a boy, I lived near the Pacific Ocean in Washington State. When my parents took me to the beach, they warned me about the undertow. They told me that if I ever got caught in the powerful currents beneath the waves, I should not fight them. By fighting, I would become exhausted and drown. A better strategy, they said, is to submit to the seaward pull of the ocean, floating on your back until you are carried to calmer waters. Then you can realign yourself with the in-going currents and swim safely to shore.

Similarly, when we fight the undertow of grief, we drown spiritually. Denying or ignoring feelings creates inner exhaustion, and along with it, depression. But honoring the pain by exploring its sources in the unconscious can be the first step toward living beyond it. There is a Hebrew phrase, *Shatuf Hawkadosh Baruch U.* Roughly translated, it means, "We are partners with God in creation." If I am God's partner, I know he wants what's best for me, but I also have a role to play. I must cooperate with the creation process by seeking God in my depths. By finding God there, I am able to accept life as it is, not as I want it to be.

Some things must be broken in order for their hidden beauty to be revealed. So it is with life. Our brokenness turns us toward God, and only by this turning can we be made whole. I think of a village known for centuries for its exquisite porcelain. The urns made in this village were especially striking. High as tables, wide as chairs, the urns drew praise around the world for their strong form and delicate beauty. According to legend, when each urn was finished there was one final step. The artist *broke it* and then put it back together with gold filigree. This last step transformed an ordinary urn into a masterpiece.[8]

Given a choice, no one would ask for brokenness. But brokenness is often what life gives us. Though this seems tragic and unfair, it can also be a blessing in disguise. Our wounds humble us and show us our need for God. They are the gold filigree that makes our character all the more valuable. Just as the Monongahela and Allegheny rivers intersect in Pittsburgh to form the Ohio, so can our confrontation with brokenness foster new dimensions of beauty within us. These confrontations are like a steep grade beneath a runner's feet or a swift current against a swimmer's stroke. They provide the resistance that fuels the process of growth.

Accepting this is liberating and empowering. It changes our perspective, enabling us to see our wounds not as problems but as possibilities. Jesus sought this perspective in Gethsemane; working through his grief advanced him toward God. This is the journey of individuation. As painful as it can be, he invites us to take it with him. When we do, we befriend our brokenness, not bemoan it, and we discover the freedom that living in acceptance brings.

MEDITATION

When acceptance is deeply rooted in us, we learn the difference between what we can change and what we can't. This knowledge opens a new world to us—the world of serenity. This world must be entered again and again.

With your eyes closed, imagine a wardrobe closet like the one C. S. Lewis describes in the *Chronicles of Narnia*. See yourself open the door of the wardrobe and step through it into an illuminating scene of beauty, peace, and joy. Entering this world, you leave behind anxiety and grief. Step through the wardrobe from alienation to love. Step from rejection to approval, from exhaustion to rest. God awaits you. Jesus said, "I am the gate" (John 10:9) Stepping through is coming home.

Use the following benediction to help accept your wounds and stay in the new world of serenity:

Everything I need I have.
Everything I am I accept.
May I find peace in God.
May I let go and love.

PRAYER

O you whose thoughts are above my thoughts,
and whose ways are above my ways, I seek you.

Only in your presence
do I let down my guard.

Your acceptance frees me
to be who I am.

No more hiding.
No more pretending.

I can rest in your love.

Though my life often seems out of control,
I need not fear,
for you are with me.

I see no cloud by day
nor pillar of fire by night.

Yet your Spirit witnesses to my spirit
that I am not alone.

Embrace me once more, gentle God,
and calm the clamor within me.

I am tired of being dissatisfied.

Trying to fill my emptiness
on my own terms exhausts me.

(continued)

(continued)

I've had enough of hurrying
and worrying
and striving.
Slow me down, Lord.

May the mind that was in Christ Jesus,
the mind of patience and peace, also be in me.

Teach me to change what I can
and leave the rest to you.

Dig the well of acceptance deep within me,
that I might love you and others fully,
having first loved the brokenness in myself. Amen.

DOING FOR OTHERS IS ANOTHER WAY OF CARING FOR YOURSELF

The Challenge of Self-Giving

If I were to name a movie that dramatizes the journey toward individuation, I would name *Rain Man*, starring Dustin Hoffman and Tom Cruise. Cruise plays Charlie Babbit, a self-absorbed young hustler who sells imported cars in Los Angeles. All he cares about is himself, and he is miserable. When his father dies early in the film, Charlie receives the shock of his life: He has been cut out of the $3 million estate. His father leaves it to Raymond, an older brother Charlie did not know existed.

Ray is an autistic savant. Institutionalized for years, he has a genius for instant mathematical calculation, but Ray throws a tantrum if someone touches him, keeps him from watching his favorite TV shows, or stops him from eating his favorite foods. Charlie abducts Ray. He hopes to manipulate Dr. Bruner, who controls the estate, into giving him half. But Charlie gets more than he bargains for as he and Ray drive from Cincinnati to Los Angeles in the family '49 Buick Roadmaster.

The two brothers bond. Charlie sees beyond Ray's oddities and discovers his humanness. In making a loving connection

Jesus answered them, "The hour has come for the Son of Man to be glorified. Very truly, I tell you, unless a grain of wheat falls into the earth and dies, it remains just a single grain; but if it dies, it bears much fruit."

JOHN 12:23–24

with him, Charlie moves from self-absorption to self-giving. He refuses the $250,000 bribe that Dr. Bruner offers him to walk away and leave Ray alone. Charlie wants custody of his older brother instead. At the hearing Charlie says, "You have to understand that when we started out together, he was only my brother in name. . . and this morning we had pancakes. . . . I made a connection." In the end, Charlie loses the custody fight but gains his soul. No longer egocentric, he is ready to receive the good gifts life offers those who love.

I believe that God wants us all to experience a similar transformation. Egocentricity comes as naturally for us as it did for Charlie Babbit. Only through spiritual attentiveness can we transcend it. Such transcendence enriches our relationships and frees our hearts, but attaining it requires a lifetime of commitment.

A war rages inside us. Though created in God's image, we are children of the earth. Light and darkness clash in our souls. Capable of both good and evil, we sometimes soar on the wings of love, but just as often we suffocate in the quicksands of fear and indifference. That's why self-giving is hard. At our best, we want to practice it, but our darker passions get in the way. We need help. The help comes from our center, the vital reservoir of integration within us.

INDIVIDUATION AND THE CROSS

Jesus relied on his center for peace and strength during the last days of his life. After his triumphal entry into Jerusalem, he sensed that his suffering and death were near. Rather than despairing, he said to his disciples, "The hour has come for the Son of Man to be glorified. Very truly, I tell you, unless a grain of wheat falls into the earth and dies, it remains just a single grain; but if it dies, it bears much fruit" (John 12:23–24). The cross and the empty tomb are reminders that he fulfilled this parable in his own self-giving. He laid down his life for the sins of the world. Salvation is offered to all because of his obedience.

Christianity without atonement is a dead religion. Alienated from God, others, and ourselves, we need a reconciliation that restores us to wholeness. If this were not so, why is the world in such a mess? And why does brokenness so often intrude into our personal lives? We cannot save ourselves. Discipline may help, but it inevitably breaks down. Help may come from good values and the best of intentions, but these also fail to produce perfect peace within or around us. We need good news as well as good advice. That's what the cross of Christ offers when seen as a means of atonement *and* as a moral example. Only grace can free us from the guilt caused by our failures and sins. Grace is God's free gift, offering forgiveness and a new beginning through the blood of Christ.

But what does the cross say about spiritual growth? If Christ is "the paradigm of the individuating ego," as Jungian analyst Edward F. Edinger suggests, the example of Christ says that growth involves giving oneself for others. A self-centered life is a stagnant life.

Edinger sees the crucifixion as a profound psychological drama. Christ's humanity is a symbol of the ego; his divinity, of the self. As a man, Christ accepts the cross as his destiny, but does so with anguish. So, too, must we accept the suffering of individuation, a suffering caused by our struggle to reconcile our inner opposites. Christ also goes to the cross as incarnate God. This is analogous to the self giving up its hiddenness and mystery in order to manifest itself in human personality.[1] "Though he was rich, yet for your sakes he became poor, so that by his poverty you might become rich" (2 Cor. 8:9).

If you feel unsettled within, it may be because of the psychological drama of the cross. Your self and your ego are competing for supremacy in your inner life. Letting go of egocentricity and embracing the self's invitation to wholeness feels like a crucifixion. You cannot be born into creativity and completeness without first dying to pride and possessiveness. Self-realization requires self-giving. The problem is, the ego denies this truth. It wants your complete allegiance, refusing to rest until you have made idols of your unfulfilled needs and desires.

The opposite of egocentricity is humility. When Jesus went to the cross, he showed humility. Rather than honoring the world's values of wealth, power, and success, he celebrated poverty, weakness, and failure. This is Christianity's ultimate contradiction: In Christ, God died a shameful death as a criminal on a cross, giving himself even for those who killed him.

The imitation of Christ does not mean martyrdom but consciousness, contends John A. Sanford. To follow Christ is to invite the light of God into one's darkness, as he did. Mystically and psychologically, he gave his life in order to share his spiritual awareness with all humanity. Sanford contends that "Christ nailed to the cross shows us the way we must go: nailed to our own process of creative change, which is something from which we cannot escape and from which we must not try to escape."

The cross teaches that we all must bear our own psychological burden of becoming conscious. It also declares that love is anything but sentimental. Love suffers. Growth toward individuation is not achieved intellectually but passionately, since, as Sanford says, "it is love that is both beautiful and painful, that opens us up to a larger consciousness, and that finally merges with divine love to ennoble the soul."[2]

Sanford highlights life's essential question: What does it mean to love? From the perspective of the cross, we see that love is different from romance. Romance is a feeling, love is a choice. Nor is love the same as affection, which waxes and wanes according to changing circumstances. Love remains the same. It stays committed to the welfare of another, no matter what. It freely gives of itself for someone else's benefit. According to psychiatrist M. Scott Peck, love is "the will to extend one's self for the purpose of nurturing one's own or another's spiritual growth."[3]

The urge to give pulsates deep within you. It comes from God, in whose image you are made. Giving is God's nature. Sunshine and mountains and flowers and rivers bear witness to this. When you give, you align yourself with the underlying rhythm of the universe and fulfill your purpose in this world.

The consequences of missing this purpose are profound. In my first pastorate, I knew a successful businessman who attended church only on Christmas and Easter. Though likable enough, he kept people at a distance and had few friends. He and his wife owned a nice home. When the man's wife died, he moved out of the home but left the furnishings untouched. His wife's clothing remained in the closets, her china in the cupboards, her jewelry on the dresser. The home stayed vacant for years. So tightly did he cling to it and all it symbolized, that he refused to sell or rent it, even when it fell into disrepair and became a favorite target for vandals. Then he got sick. When I visited him in the hospital, his home was much on his mind. The thought of dying and being separated from his property and possessions unnerved him. To the end, he clung to them like a child clings to a security blanket. Seldom have I seen a more traumatic death.

By contrast, Dr. Elihu Wing, Jr., a successful physician, retired with the material rewards of years of practicing medicine. But rather than rest on his laurels, he joined me and twenty-two others on a mission trip to La Romana in the Dominican Republic. We spent a week working at a hospital for the indigent population of that area. Dr. Wing also visited the impoverished communities where the sugar cane workers and their families live, and he provided medical care to the children. When he retired a year later, he wanted to go back again. Whether with a stethoscope around his neck or a bag of cement in his hands, he practiced self-giving. To this day, he speaks of the immeasurable spiritual rewards of doing so.

SACRIFICES OF THE LIBERATED HEART

It takes an independent person to give in imitation of Christ, who laid down his life expecting nothing in return. There is a big difference between this spontaneous generosity and the addictive loving that springs from dependency. If I need you in order to feel good about myself, I place my life in your hands. I become what Fritz Kunkel calls a "Clinging Vine," expecting you to make me happy instead of finding happiness within. Thus I allow you to control my moods. Rather than being my own person, I become your puppet. This is dependency, not love, and it leads to brokenness.

Christ's self-giving was different from dependency. It came from his center, from the presence of God in him. He had nothing to lose because he surrendered everything to this presence. Surrendering meant forgiving those who mocked and beat him. It meant placing the welfare of others above his own and setting aside his fears in order to alleviate theirs. These were outward signs of his inward offering of himself to God.

Our problem is that we often think of giving ourselves to God as something negative. We resist because we must let go of too much—our pride, selfishness, and lust. Jesus' example convinces me that I need to change this attitude in order to grow. Imitating him cannot be mechanical; it must come from the heart. Following Jesus in action begins with sharing his consciousness. As Jung said, "Christ can indeed be imitated even to the point of stigmatization without the imitator coming anywhere near the ideal or its meaning. For it is not a question of an imitation that leaves a man [or woman] unchanged and makes him [or her] into a mere artifact, but of realizing the ideal on one's own account—*Deo concedente*—in one's own individual life."[4]

The cross cultivates heroic faith; the crucifixion declares that suffering is redemptive. Christianity teaches that, in Jesus, God suffered for us, and now suffers with us, no matter how abandoned we feel. Our crucifixion experiences advance the process of individuation. There is something empowering about the kind of faith that survives the experience of feeling utterly forsaken. By persevering in faith when we feel crucified by life, we participate in our own transformation. Our crucifixion experiences create the vulnerability necessary to receive grace. We realize that we can't make it on our own and must turn to God for help. Often help comes through a growing awareness that the resources we need to face our crises and solve our problems are within us. Crucifixion experiences are redemptive when they force us to rely on these inner resources, for such reliance fosters spiritual growth and propels the individuation process.

Such heroic people as St. Francis of Assisi, Albert Schweitzer, Helen Keller, Dorothy Day, Mohandas Gandhi, and Martin Luther King, Jr., gave out of their suffering, as Jesus did. Rather than become cynical or embittered when life hurt them, they maintained their commitment to love. They could not have done so without moral courage, depth of faith, and strength of character. Their way of offering themselves for others may seem naive to the world, but it resonates in the depths of God. This is what the apostle Paul called the foolishness of the cross. It makes no sense to those who are perishing in their unconsciousness, but to those thirsting for individuation, it is the power and wisdom of God (1 Cor. 1:18). Such persistent self-giving can restore lost self-respect, heal broken relationships, and subvert the world's cruelty with a powerful spiritual wisdom.

A man named John joined the army during the Korean War. John was so ill-suited for military life that he became the laughingstock of his platoon, and even the sergeant made his life hell. One day, some of the other men played a joke on John. They obtained a dummy grenade, which the sergeant told everyone was live. He handed it to one of the men, who pulled the pin and fumbled with it, letting it drop at John's feet. As quick as lightning, John fell on top of the grenade, burying it in his stomach. Seconds passed. No one moved. When there was no explosion, John realized it was all a joke. He had been humiliated again. But when he looked up, no one was laughing. The sergeant dusted him off and helped him to his feet, as the other men looked on with new respect. His courageous self-giving had won their admiration. Never again did they laugh at his bumbling. [5]

It takes a centered person to respond as John did. He triumphed over adversity by drawing on his inner resources of love. In the process, he saved not only his own dignity but also the dignity of the entire platoon. This kind of centeredness is like the mustard seed, which Jesus compared to the kingdom of God: it seems small but gives birth to a magnificent tree (Matt. 13:31–32). We are all misfits in some way, there are hidden reserves of strength and courage in us. We draw on these reserves by remaining connected to the higher consciousness of the self amid our crucifixion experiences. So connected, we give of ourselves out of our own deep humanity, honoring the humanity in others, undeterred by the risks and sacrifices required.

Such giving inspires hope. When I see a cross displayed at a hospital, soup kitchen, or shelter for the homeless, I marvel at how Jesus' example has lived on for centuries, radiating through his people to bring compassion to the needy. Love endures. It motivates efforts to comfort the sorrowing, heal the broken, and liberate the oppressed. Nothing can ultimately defeat love, though it suffers many losses in a fallen world. Wherever practiced, it bears witness to God's presence and affirms life's goodness.

Most of us need to learn this lesson again and again. Growing spiritually means trusting in love's power, even when it seems weak and ineffectual. We can maintain this trust only when grounded in our center, the place where we encounter God as Jesus did. Such an encounter is necessary if we are to answer the call of the cross to self-giving and individuation. Hope triumphs when our answer is yes.

MEDITATION

Create an image in your mind of your favorite musical instrument. Without such instruments, music remains a theory, a silent possibility unable to express itself. So it is with God's love: if not expressed by human instruments, it remains hidden and unknown.

Meditate on the ways God can speak through you. You are an instrument created to play love's redeeming and liberating melodies. By imitating God's self-giving in Christ, you make love concrete. Each time you lend a helping hand, contribute to a worthy cause, stand up for a moral ideal, or otherwise use your gifts and resources to improve the lives of others, you become an instrument of God's peace. Using the prayer of St. Francis of Assisi to focus your meditation, open yourself to God's presence and surrender to the ideals that the prayer celebrates:

> Lord, make me an instrument of your peace.
> Where there is hatred, let me sow love;
> where there is injury, pardon;
> where there is doubt, faith;
> where there is despair, hope;
> where there is darkness, light;
> where there is sadness, joy.
> O divine Master, grant that I may not so much seek
> to be consoled, as to console,
> to be understood, as to understand,
> to be loved, as to love,
> for it is in giving that we receive;
> it is in pardoning that we are pardoned;
> it is in dying that we are born to eternal life.

PRAYER

Giver of all good gifts,
I marvel at your generosity.

Each refreshing morning,
each blazing sunset,
each cool mist in the deep woods
comes from your hand.

I do not take this for granted;
the world is full of wonder because of your provisions.
I stand in awe of your goodness.

Though life can be both wonderful and awful,
both full of grace and full of pain,
it is all yours, loving God.

You include everything in your embrace.
Embrace me, too, I pray.

I want to feel close to you,
as close as I feel to my own breath,
to my own heartbeat,
to my own most intimate thoughts.

When you reveal your presence deep within me,
I know I am part of your good creation.

You have given me so much—
eyes to see,
ears to hear,

(continued)

a heart to feel,
a mind to think.

I have been blessed with material abundance
and spiritual riches in Christ.

Teach me to share, O God.

Show me what I have to give,
and help me offer it to others in love.

Cleanse my heart of ulterior motives.

May I imitate you in my relationships,
wanting another's happiness more than my own,
giving not to receive
but to celebrate your presence within me.

I open myself to you in this moment,
that I may not love in needy or addictive ways,
but in the freedom and self-giving
that your Spirit inspires. Amen.

YOU CAN'T STOP THE WAVES, BUT YOU CAN LEARN TO SURF

The Challenge of Resurrection

The Christian gospel does not end in death. I have known this for as long as I can remember, but depth psychology broadened my understanding of what resurrection means. Our crucifixion experiences—our most painful defeats and losses—can give rise to spiritual growth. On the inward journey, the old must die in order for the new to be born. Resurrection is not only an anticipated future event. It can also be a present reality, a gateway to individuation.

June 1994 has become for me a parable of this truth. On the third day of that month, a Friday, my grandmother died. Losing Neñe, my only living grandparent, was like losing part of myself. Neñe was a free spirit. Her distinctive Greek accent, infectious laugh, and unconquerable love of life made her special. She never refused an invitation to a party. Wherever she was and whatever she did, she had a good time. Not once did I see her embarrassed or intimidated by any situation. To be with her was to experience enchantment and passion, adventure and drama.

In my darkest moments I hear Neñe's voice saying, "Always be proud of who and what you are. Never, ever be ashamed.

But the angel said to the women, "Do not be afraid; I know that you are looking for Jesus who was crucified. He is not here; for he has been raised, as he said. Come, see the place where he lay."

MATTHEW 28:5–6

Be yourself, no matter what. Remember that success is not about wealth or fame or power or knowledge, but about inner strength and authenticity. Pay no attention to your critics. What matters is not what they think of you, but what you think of yourself. Don't be afraid to feel life deeply, express your emotions, or take risks in pursuit of your dreams. Most of all, always keep fighting, and never give up."

Now she was gone. It didn't matter that it was time; that she was ninety-four; that she had had a wonderful life. That she lived in her own home until the end. It still hurt. My heart was heavy for days. I needed a spiritual resurrection, and I got one. On June 24th, exactly three weeks after Neñe died, my first child was born.

Evan John Howard came into the world by Caesarean section. After nearly sixteen years of marriage and a long struggle with infertility, Carol and I were finally parents. Temperature charts, ovulation kits, and drug therapy did not help us. Only when we quit medical treatments in despair did nature take its course. Grace succeeded where infertility specialists failed.

Our son's birth turned tears of sorrow into tears of joy. I have never felt such a reversal of emotions. We received gifts, cards, and phone calls from friends and family members across the country. My congregation was ecstatic; my neighbors were ecstatic; everyone was ecstatic! It felt like a miracle. Looking into my son's eyes, I experienced an emotional resurrection. I knew, as I had never known before, the reality of grace.

THE INNER MEANING OF THE RESURRECTION

I wonder if Jesus experienced a similar reversal of emotions. On the first Easter he went from the tomb's bondage to the dawn's deliverance, from night to light. His woundedness and waiting became healing and rejoicing. The angel's words to the women sounded the note of triumph, "Do not be afraid; I know that you are looking for Jesus who was crucified. He is not here; for he has been raised, as he said. Come, see the place where he lay" (Matt. 28:5–6). The inner meaning of these words is that Jesus' spiritual journey continued. If it had not, Christianity would not have been founded; there would have been no gospel and no church. Raised from the dead by God, Jesus' life took on eternal significance.

The resurrection not only validated his teachings and transformed his crucifixion from a defeat to a victory—it also vindicated his faith and increased his awareness of God's presence and power. In this latter sense, experiencing resurrection as a life event is essential to personal wholeness. According to depth psychology, the specific details about the resurrection are unimportant; what matters is whether resurrection happens here and now in a person's psyche. While I rejoice in Easter's proclamation of death's defeat and its promise of eternal life. I yearn for spiritual resurrection now. This is what integrative faith offers me. In Jung's language, Christ is a symbol of the self.[1] He "did not merely *symbolize* wholeness, but, as a psychic phenomenon, he *was* wholeness."[2]

Jesus' resurrection teaches timeless truths about the process of inner development. Jung emphasizes this in his essay "On Resurrection," in which he interprets Easter in psychological terms. As an archetype of the self, Jesus cannot remain in the tomb; the self is immortal and can only be fully realized in eternity. The resurrection represents the triumph of "the greater personality in every individual,"[3] the victory of the God-image within over disintegration and darkness.

But these forces cannot be easily subdued. Their power brings brokenness and despair to countless lives. Watch the evening news and see the pain caused by disintegration and darkness. Behind every story of exploitation, corruption, and violence is the human spirit at war with itself. Where does healing begin? With inner transformation, symbolized by the resurrection.

Just as Jesus was raised from death to life, so can disintegrated individuals experience spiritual awakening. "If psychologically the death of Christ on the cross. . . is the death of our old egocentric personality," writes John A. Sanford, "then the resurrection is the emergence in us of a new consciousness, rooted in the creative Center within us."[4] This new consciousness evolves when "the old person dies and the new person lives through participation in a personality larger than the ego."[5]

The spiritual journey is a quest for this new consciousness. To be a spiritual person is to be attentive to the process of death and resurrection. But attentiveness often reveals the need for change, and no one changes easily. You cannot be born into the new consciousness unless you pay the price of surrendering the old one. Rigid value systems must become more flexible. Negative self-images must give way to positive ones. Prejudices, fears, and dishonesties must yield to the higher urgings of love.

Most of us learn this the hard way. It can take years of inner turmoil before we are ready for a change of consciousness. For a long time I felt like a failure as a pastor, because I thought of success in worldly terms—growing membership, flourishing programs, and an expanding budget. But I have served small churches. My two pastorates have been in congregations that have declined numerically over the years but still maintain large buildings. Ministry in this context affords few tangible signs of success. Feelings of inadequacy intruded and I tried to meet impossible standards. I had to hit bottom emotionally before this old consciousness could die and a new consciousness could be born. Resurrection came when I began valuing quality more than quantity in ministry. Only when relationships, not results, became my central focus did I start feeling better about myself and my work. Interestingly enough, that's also when my congregations began to grow.

THE HIDDEN BENEFITS OF PERSONAL CRISIS

The old consciousness seldom dies easily. It clings to life with the tenacity of a drowning man clinging to a rescue line. We let it. The old consciousness is familiar. It feels comfortable and secure. Letting it die means facing the unknown, embracing something new and different, taking a risk. So we keep resuscitating the old, even if it has outlived its usefulness and become a source of brokenness within us. We may need a crisis to help us trust the mystery of resurrection. When stretched to the breaking point, we come face to face with our dysfunctional ways of thinking and acting. These must die in order for wholeness to be born.

If we want to be whole, we need to know when change is necessary. Feelings of stagnation, anxiety, depression, or meaninglessness may indicate that our old consciousness no longer works. The survival strategies that brought us this far have broken down. Although frightening, a unique opportunity arises from the ashes of your unsettledness. It's the opportunity to listen to our soul.

The soul speaks in whispers, not shouts, and it never offers quick fixes. This is why many people miss its message. The soul calls us back to our center in God. It speaks through life's struggles, inviting us to rely on grace, grow in patience, and learn from pain. This means giving up naive ideas about finding ultimate fulfillment and security in life. As our consciousness becomes more spiritual, we stop resenting our dark nights of the soul, but instead respect them as our greatest teachers. They point the way toward individuation.

By listening to our turmoil, we discover where we need to grow. Since much turmoil is rooted in alienation from love, we must discern what love requires in our relationships and circumstances. This is the primary task of the spiritual journey. We see light in our darkness as we learn to love as God loves. This integrative loving is the imitation of Christ. It is seldom without pain but never without hope. Practicing it requires a resurrection perspective, an inner confidence that when an old consciousness dies, a new one arises to illumine the way toward wholeness.

Psychiatrist Frederic Flach calls this resilience. He contends that the movement from brokenness to wholeness is mandated by nature. People adapt and grow according to a cyclical process of "disruption and re-integration," which begins when stressful conditions create "bifurcation points" all along the life cycle. Persevering through these times of stress develops personality traits such as creativity, independence, self-respect, and tolerance for pain. Those who have these traits rebound from crisis to build a better, more constructive future.[6]

Medical research supports Flach's conclusions. There is a flow toward wholeness at the center of life, often called the *vis medicatrix naturae*, "the healing power of nature." This natural "superwisdom" favors life, not death. That postmortem examinations often reveal traces of diseases that the deceased conquered without knowing it is evidence of this. Belief in this flow toward wholeness is also a principle of depth psychology. According to Jung, "there is an ever-present archetype of wholeness"[6] in each person. Wholeness is both a potential and a capacity. As such, it cannot be earned; it must be rediscovered as one's original condition. This rediscovery "may never be perceived at all until a consciousness illuminated by conversion recognizes it in the figure of Christ. As a result of this *anamnesis* the original state of oneness with the God-image is restored. It brings about an integration, a bridging of the split in the personality caused by the instincts striving apart in different and mutually contradictory directions."[8]

AN INVITATION TO BEGIN ANEW

Consider the activities of the risen Christ. He sought to share with his followers the wholeness he found in the resurrection consciousness. But he had difficulty penetrating their defenses; they were too filled with doubts and fears. He had to persist. Adopting the resurrection consciousness means trusting in a transformation still in process, leaving the future to God. This can be terrifying. Thus, to Mary Magdelene and the other women at the tomb, he said, "Do not be afraid" (Matt. 28:10).

Because the resurrection consciousness is not about blind faith but about disciplined reflection, he allowed Thomas his doubts, and called "blessed" future Thomases, "who have not seen and yet have come to believe" (John 20:29). The resurrection consciousness is also redemptive. Peter discovered this on the beach by the Sea of Tiberias. There he had breakfast with the risen Lord and received forgiveness for denying him. Cleopas and his friend on the Emmaus road learned that the resurrection consciousness is expressed in community. Jesus walked with them and stayed for dinner in their home. Only in their togetherness did he break the bread, give it to them, and allow them to recognize him. Later, Jesus revealed himself to Saul of Tarsus on the Damascus road. Brought from fanaticism to faith, from death to life, Saul became Paul, "apostle of the heart set free," a phrase coined by New Testament scholar F. F. Bruce.

Jesus used all of these encounters to help his followers connect with their souls. He wanted them to integrate their spirituality into their everyday lives by imitating him. This meant surrendering to the resurrection consciousness as he had. Fritz Kunkel says that "Easter, rebirth, the new phase of creation, is either a convincing inner experience which changes our character and our life, or it is nothing at all."[9] Jesus' followers changed the world because God's victorious love first changed them.

A few years ago *Time* magazine ran an article about Larry Trapp, a disabled Grand Dragon of the Ku Klux Klan, and how he had harassed a Jewish clergyman named Michael Weisser. Trapp sent Weisser anti-Semitic hate mail in an attempt to drive him out of town. Weisser responded by reminding Trapp that the Nazis, whom Trapp idolized, had sent the disabled to concentration camps.

When the two men finally spoke, Weisser refused to return hate for hate. Instead, he offered Trapp a ride to the grocery store. This gesture of kindness led to reconciliation and friendship. Weisser and his wife went to Trapp's home with a peace offering of a silver ring. "As we walked in I touched his hand and he burst into tears," recalled Weisser. "He didn't know we were bringing the ring, and he had two silver swastika rings on, one on each hand. He took the two rings off and said, 'I want you to take these rings; they just symbolize hatred and evil, and I want them out of my life.' Julie gave him the other ring and put it on his finger." [10]

Trapp's consciousness changed that day. He surrendered to love, had a spiritual awakening, and became a new person. The resurrection declares that this can happen to anyone. Love, embodied in Jesus, suffers many defeats in the world and in our lives, but the resurrection promises that love will rise again. To adopt the resurrection consciousness is to live in hope of this rising. It is to trust in love's eventual triumph, even when its enemies threaten and assail.

SKILLS OF TRANSFORMED LIVING

The hope of resurrection nurtures inner strength. Believing we can come back from our defeats, as Jesus came back from death, sustains us amid them. We begin seeing defeats as temporary. We maintain our composure and search for solutions to our problems. We resist the allure of cynicism, negativity, and resentment. Most of all, we remain friends with ourselves. Rather than engage in self-condemnation, which produces shame and guilt, we accept God's forgiveness and invitation to new life.

Surrendering to the resurrection consciousness is an acquired skill. We know we are learning it when we develop a positive inner dialogue. This means telling ourselves, "I will persevere through this crisis and it will make me a better person." "Nothing can happen to me that I cannot endure with God's help." "Yes, I made a mistake, but I will learn from it and deepen in my appreciation of grace." "This loss feels unbearable; I must grieve. But in waiting out the darkness until the light of God shines through, I will become a more sensitive, caring person."

Life sometimes leaves us bruised and broken, but Christ's resurrection promises that grace eventually triumphs and that we will rise again, but not as the same person we were before.

Resurrection means letting go of our former identity and connecting with life and God in new ways. This fosters inner transformation. Death and rebirth force us to explore our depths until we encounter our real self, whom God loves. Discovering this love, we receive each day as a gift and participate in our own growth process. Life becomes a profound mystery. Rather than try to understand it, we savor and celebrate it, humbled by its sorrows but sustained by its joys.

A popular poster from some years ago captured the spirit of the resurrection consciousness. It showed an eastern guru with gray hair and a long beard balanced on one foot on a surfboard. He was wearing only a small loincloth as he coasted down a large wave. At the bottom of the poster were the words, "You can't stop the waves, but you can learn to surf."[11] Those are good words to remember when we are buffeted by the defeats and losses of life. Each represents a death experience, and we can't stop them from happening. What we can do, however, is remain centered in the resurrection consciousness. This means waiting and listening and trusting, as Jesus did for three days in the tomb, until the night passes and our spirits rise again.

This waiting period is a good time to dream. Though some consider dreaming naive, they forget that progress cannot be made without it. It is important to dream in all the moments of your life, in darkness as well as light. Once you stop dreaming, you stop living. Nurturing the dream of wholeness means leaving the familiar behind and traveling to unknown lands of challenge where resiliency must be learned. Often we find new depth and resources within ourselves in these lands. Failing to dream of wholeness, we languish in the tomb of indifference, immobilized by fear and inhibitions.

When we feel beaten and discouraged, it may help to remember those who embody the resurrection spirit. Think of pianist

Leon Fleisher performing publicly again after his right hand had been immobilized for seventeen years by carpal tunnel syndrome; British novelist John Creasey receiving 753 rejection slips before publishing 564 books; and American cyclist Greg Lemond coming back from a near-fatal gunshot wound to win the Tour de France. Think of Paula Hawkins rising to serve as a U.S. senator from Florida after being sexually abused as a child; Napalese mountain guide Sungdare overcoming snow-blindness and frostbite to become the first man to conquer Mt. Everest three times; and Vietnam double-amputee Bill Demby playing basketball on artificial legs in a nationwide television commercial.

Resurrection is a divorced mother of three devotedly raising her children as a single parent. It is an alcoholic father determined to stay sober and redeem the mistakes of the past. It is the man or woman who works for years at an unsatisfying job without engaging in self-pity. It is you and I remaining centered in God amid the stresses of our lives. It is a triumph over adversity, a relentless spirit of endurance, a determination to beat the odds, come what may.

A MAN FOR THE AGES

More than anyone else, Jesus Christ embodies the resurrection spirit. What his enemies thought was the end of him was only the beginning. Through resurrection he became a model of wholeness for all time. Albert Schweitzer concludes in his famous book, *The Quest of the Historical Jesus,* that Jesus "comes to us as One unknown." [12] This means that he represents the unknown part of ourselves, the part that yearns for freedom and renewal, for integration and intimacy. We are fascinated by him because the same Spirit that lived in him lives in us. This Spirit connects us not only with eternity but also with our best selves. Because the Spirit is within us yet beyond us, we gravitate toward people who bring it near, Jesus being chief among them.

Imitating Jesus means adopting his consciousness. It means surrendering to God and to love in the present moment and journeying toward transfigured life. What we become on this journey cannot be measured by external standards. It is a continual process of inner growth; only God knows the outcome. We follow

Jesus because he was, in Marcus J. Borg's phrase, a "spirit person," one who invites us to move from "secondhand religion" to "firsthand religion." He takes us from believing doctrines about God "into a transforming relationship with the same Spirit that he himself knew, and into a community whose social vision was shaped by the core value of compassion." [13]

To integrate faith *in* Jesus with the faith *of* Jesus is to find the fullness of life—life centered in love for God, others, and self. Such centeredness promises no easy answers. Integrative faith celebrates paradox and ambiguity for their value in soulmaking. Each person soars to the heights of joy and plunges to the depths of despair; laughter and tears sensitize the heart. Only God knows the meaning of it all. But the spiritual quest is about seeking meaning in the moment. It is about listening to one's depths, feeling one's emotions, honoring one's personhood. It is about silence and patience and perseverance. It is about attentiveness to the eternal in the midst of time.

The quest enriches life. Relationships deepen; cherished memories multiply; inner peace increases. Problems do not disappear, but God's presence provides hope for solving them. A spiritual perspective changes everything. It informs all experiences. Success becomes an opportunity for sharing. Mistakes and failures become teachers of humility and mediators of grace. Sunsets, moonbeams, and rainbows become messengers of wonder. Life is still beautiful and painful; precious moments still pass too quickly, never to be recaptured; tragedies still happen and hearts still break. But a spiritual perspective seeks God in it all, and God is there. To affirm God's presence is to open oneself to transformation. Jesus did this, and the world has never forgotten him. Following him is the challenge of a lifetime. Let the challenge begin.

MEDITATION

Close your eyes and cover them with your hands. As you do this, you will shut out all light. Let the darkness symbolize death. Meditate on the truth that death is part of life, inevitable but never final on the spiritual journey. As winter precedes spring, and as night turns to morning, death gives birth to resurrection life. You have probably experienced the death of relationships, dreams, ideals, loved ones, mental or physical abilities, beliefs, and many other things.

As you meditate in the darkness, reflect on your losses and ask God to help you accept them. Move deep within yourself. Feel your feelings. Allow yourself to grieve. Ask for the strength and grace to let go of what you cannot change and get on with your life. Wait patiently in the stillness, letting it speak to you of hope and healing.

When ready, remove your hands from your eyes while keeping them closed. Be present to the light that now shines into your darkness. Meditate on the ways God is bringing forth new life out of the deaths you have experienced, and present the unsurrendered parts of yourself to God for transformation.

PRAYER

O God of the eternal sunrise and the invincible springtime,
I am alive in you. Fully alive.

Because of your Spirit's presence within me,
I need not fear death. Yet I do fear.

I tremble when I contemplate the death of a dream
or a cherished relationship,
the death of a beloved friend
or a part of my own body or soul.

Death devastates me. It brings confusion to my mind
and anguish to my heart; it makes me weep.

O God of resurrection,
I cry to you in my vulnerability and woundedness.

I easily forget that the old must die
in order for the new to be born.

Rather than embrace the birth process,
I shun it in the hope of avoiding its pain.

Even when old ways of thinking and feeling and acting
no longer work, I cling to them
because they are familiar and comfortable.

Teach me the truth of the seasons, O God.
May I remember that there is
a time for birth and a time for growth,
a time for maturity and a time for death,

just as the year progresses
from spring to summer to autumn to winter.

Make me attentive to the seasons of my spirit.

Help me listen to each emotion
and show reverence for each mood I feel.

Remind me amid darkness and death
that resurrection will eventually come,
bringing light and warmth,
as surely as the spring
melts winter's ice and snow.

I need a springtime and an Easter, O God,
not once a year, but every day.

Lead me toward transformation.
Come to me now and awaken an alleluia in my heart.
I wait for you in hope. Amen.

NOTES

PREFACE

1. Thomas R. Kelly, *A Testament of Devotion* (New York: Harper & Brothers, 1941), 17.

CHAPTER ONE

1. Joseph Campbell, with Bill Moyers, *The Power of Myth* (New York: Doubleday, 1988), 117–118.
2. Rudolf Otto, *The Idea of the Holy* (New York: Oxford University Press, 1958), 155–159.
3. Marcus J. Borg, *Jesus: A New Vision* (San Francisco: HarperSanFrancisco, 1987), 40.
4. Ibid., 27, 87.
5. Ibid., 44–45.
6. Ibid., 97, 111.
7. Ibid., 102.
8. Borg, *Meeting Jesus Again for the First Time* (San Francisco: HarperSanFrancisco, 1993), 88.
9. Evelyn Underhill, *Mysticism* (New York: Penguin, 1955), 121.
10. John A. Sanford, *The Kingdom Within Leader's Guide* (San Francisco: HarperSanFrancisco, 1991), 48.
11. Sanford, Mystical, *Christianity: A Psychological Commentary on the Gospel of John* (New York: Crossroad, 1993), 169–170.
12. C. G. Jung, "AION: Researches into the Phenomenology of

the Self," *Collected Works of C. G. Jung* [hereafter *CW*], vol. 9:2 (Princeton, N.J.: Princeton University Press, 1959). Also "A Study in the Process of Individuation," *CW* 9:1, 290–354.

13. Thomas à Kempis, *The Imitation of Christ,* trans. William C. Creasy (Notre Dame, Ind.: Ave Maria, 1989), p. 65.

14. E. J. Tinsley, "Imitation of Christ," *The Westminster Dictionary of Christian Spirituality,* ed. Gordon S. Wakefield (Philadelphia: Westminster, 1983), 209.

15. Thomas R. Kelly, *A Testament of Devotion* (New York: Harper and Row, 1941), 42.

CHAPTER TWO

1. A. C. Thiselton, "Truth," *The New International Dictionary of the New Testament,* ed. Colin Brown, 3 vols. (Grand Rapids, Mich.: Zondervan, 1975–78), 3:874–901.

2. Jung, "Psychological Types," *CW* 6, 590.

3. Paul Tillich, *The Shaking of the Foundations* (New York: Scribner, 1948), 162.

4. Tillich, *The Courage to Be* (New Haven: Yale University Press, 1952), 32.

5. Rollo May, *The Courage to Create* (New York: W. W. Norton, 1975), 3–4.

6. Sanford, *Mystical Christianity,* 193.

CHAPTER THREE

1. Timothy Brook, *Quelling the People* (New York: Oxford University Press, 1992), p. 177; Yi Mu and Mark V. Thompson, *Crisis at Tiananmen* (San Francisco: China Books and Periodicals, 1989), p. 94.

2. Gerd Theissen, *Sociology of Early Palestinian Christianity,* trans. John Bowden (Philadelphia: Fortress, 1978), p. 42.

3. Borg, *Meeting Jesus Again for the First Time,* pp. 50–58.

4. Jung, "The Development of Personality," *CW* 17, 317.

CHAPTER FOUR

1. Gerald G. May, *Addiction and Grace* (San Francisco: Harper and Row, 1988), pp. 3–5.
2. Jung, "Psychology and Religion: West and East." *CW* 11 (New York: Pantheon, 1958), 344.

3. Sanford, *Mystical Christianity,* p. 195.
4. Fritz Kunkel, *Creation Continues: A Psychological Interpretation of the Gospel of Matthew* (New York: Paulist, 1987), p. 53.
5. Everett L. Shostrom, *Man, the Manipulator* (Nashville: Abingdon, 1967), 52.
6. Kempis, *The Imitation of Christ*, p. 74.
7. *John of the Cross, Selected Writings*, ed. Kieran Kavanaugh (New York: Paulist, 1987), p. 71.
8. Ibid, p. 722. See also Paul De Jaegher, *An Anthology of Christian Mysticism,* trans. Donald Attwater et al (Springfield, Ill.: Templegate, 1977), p. 114.

CHAPTER FIVE

1. Donald Robert Perry Marquis, *Chapters for the Orthodox* (1934), chap. 11.
2. Rufus Jones, *New Eyes for Invisibles* (New York: Macmillan, 1943), 50–55).
3. *Fritz Kunkel: Selected Writings,* ed. John A. Sanford (New York: Paulist, 1984), 315.
4. Sanford, *Mystical Christianity,* 250–60.

CHAPTER SIX

1. Carole Hyatt and Linda Gottlieb, *When Smart People Fail* (New York: Penguin, 1988), 207.
2. Jung, "Paracelsus as Spiritual Phenomenon" (1942), "Alchemical Studies" (1967), *CW* 13, 155.
3. Kunkel, *Creation Continues,* 63.
4. Jung, *Psyche and Symbol,* ed. Violet S. de Laszlo (Garden City, N.J.), Doubleday, 1958), 8.

5. Sanford, *The Kingdom Within* (San Francisco: Harper and Row, 1987), 35.
6. Garrison Keillor, *Lake Wobegon Days* (New York: Viking, 1985), 337.
7. Bani Shorter and Fred Plaut, *A Critical Dictionary of Jungian Analysis* (New York: Routledge, 1986), 79.
8. Jung, *Psyche and Symbol,* 24.
9. Gabriel Fackre, *The Christian Story* (Grand Rapids, Mich.: Eardmans, 1978), 106.
10. Richard E. Byrd, *Alone* (New York: Putnam, 1938), 116–118.

CHAPTER SEVEN

1. David G. Myers, "Pursuing Happiness," *Psychology Today* (July/August 1993), 34.
2. Morton T. Kelsey, *Healing and Christianity* (New York: Harper and Row, 1973), 54.
3. Sanford, *The Kingdom Within* (San Francisco: Harper and Row, 1987), 15–25.
4. Jung, "The Relations Between the Ego and the Unconscious," *Two Essays on Analytical Psychology, in CW* 7 (1953/1966), 267.
5. Sanford's introduction to Kunkel's "The Origin and Nature of Egocentricity" in *Fritz Kunkel: Selected Writings* (New York: Paulist, 1984), 65–66.
6. Ibid., 70.
7. Christina Feldman and Jack Kornfield, eds., *Stories of the Spirit, Stories of the Heart* (New York: HarperCollins, 1991), 28–30.
8. Henri J. M. Nouwen, *The Wounded Healer* (Garden City, N.Y.: Image Books, 1972), 92.

CHAPTER EIGHT

1. Edward Paul Cohn, "Finding Yourself at the Red Sea Place," *Pulpit Digest* 74 (September/October 1993), 33.
2. Jung, *Symbols of Transformation,* trans R.F.C. Hull, *CW* 5 (Princeton, N.J.: Princeton University Press, 1990), 205.
3. Ibid., 171.

4. Kunkel, *Creation Continues,* 123.
5. Campbell, *The Hero with a Thousand Faces* (Princeton, N.J.: Princeton University Press, 1949), 29.
6. Carol S. Pearson, *The Hero Within: Six Archetypes We Live By* (San Francisco: HarperSanFrancisco, 1989), 1.

CHAPTER NINE

1. Judith Viorst, *Necessary Losses* (New York: Ballantine, 1986), 301.
2. Kunkel, *Creation Continues,* 260.
3. Ibid., 260.
4. Jung, *Modern Man in Search of a Soul,* trans. W. S. Dell and Cary F. Baynes (New York: Harcourt Brace Jovanovich, 1933), 236–37.
5. Jung, "Commentary on the Secret of the Golden Flower," in *Psyche and Symbol,* ed. Violet de Laszlo (Garden City, N.Y.: Doubleday, 1958), 312–313.
6. Jung, "Psychology and Religion," *Psychology and Region: West and East, CW* 11 (1958/1969), 138.
7. Kempis, *The Imitation of Christ,* 103.
8. Robert J. Kriegel and Louis Patler. *If It Ain't Broke . . . Break It!* (New York: Warner Books, 1991), vii.

CHAPTER TEN

1. Edward F. Edinger, *Ego and Archetype* (Baltimore: Pelican, 1973), 152.
2. Sanford, *Mystical Christianity,* 328–329.
3. M. Scott Peck, *The Road Less Traveled* (New York: Simon and Schuster, 1978), 81.
4. Jung, "Psychology and Alchemy," *CW* 12 (1953/1968), 7.
5. Arthur Tennies, *A Church for Sinners, Seekers, and Sundry Non-Saints* (Nashville: Abingdon, 1974), 86.

CHAPTER ELEVEN

1. Jung, "Christ, a Symbol of the Self," *Psyche and Symbol,* ed. Violet S. de Laszlo (Garden City, N.Y.: Anchor, 1958), 35.

2. Ibid., 52.
3. Jung, "On Resurrection," in *Psychology and Western Religion,* trans R.F.C. Hull (Princeton, N.J.: Princeton University Press, 1984), 249.
4. Sanford, Mystical Christianity, 329.
5. Ibid., 329.
6. Frederic Flach, *Resilience* (New York: Fawcett Colombine, 1988), xi–xii.
7. Jung, *Psyche and Symbol,* 38.
8. Ibid., 38.
9. Kunkel, *Creation Continues,* 276.
10. "The Cantor and the Klansman," *Time* (February 17, 1992), 14–16.
11. Jack Kornfield, *A Path with Heart* (New York: Bantam, 1993), 113.
12. Albert Schweitzer, *The Quest of the Historical Jesus* (New York: Macmillan, 1961), 403.
13. Borg, *Meeting Jesus Again for the First Time,* 30, 87, 119.

QUESTIONS FOR REFLECTION AND DISCUSSION

CHAPTER ONE

1. How do you respond to the phrase "follow your bliss"? Do you agree or disagree that Jesus did this? How might the idea of following your bliss be applied to your Christian experience?
2. Describe your spiritual life. Do you feel that you are growing, stagnating, or somewhere in between? How does the idea of the imitation of Christ speak to you?
3. Discuss the concept of integrative faith. Why is it necessary to have the faith *of* Jesus as well as faith *in* Jesus to be "centered in God"?
4. What implications do Marcus J. Borg's insights into the spirituality of Jesus have for Christians today?
5. That Jesus loved God, others, and self as a unity is a major theme in this book. How might the practice of this integrative love free a person? Why are one-dimensional forms of love unable to inspire this freedom in its fullness?
6. This book suggests that both the spirituality of Jesus and Carl Jung's psychology of individuation are paths of transformation. How might the Jungian concepts presented in this chapter be helpful to Christians who want to grow spiritually?

CHAPTER TWO

1. How is seeking the truth about God related to finding the personal truths that give meaning to your life? In what sense was

Jesus a seeker of truth when he sat among the teachers in the temple at age twelve?

2. Why is it so hard for us to be honest with ourselves? How do evasion and denial, whether subtle or blatant, inhibit spiritual growth? How might listening to one's dreams promote honesty?

3. Reflect on the Jungian concept of the *persona*. What are some of the masks we wear and why? What are the consequences of over-identifying with the roles one plays?

4. How can a balance be struck between acknowledging one's inner hypocrisy and being too hard on oneself? What spiritual resources are needed to confront the Pharisee within without being overwhelmed by guilt?

5. Psychologist Rollo May has said that courage "is the foundation that underlies and gives reality to all other virtues and personal values." Do you agree? Why or why not?

6. What is the difference between knowledge of the head and knowledge of the heart? Why is a deep inner knowing of the truth a prerequisite of personal freedom?

CHAPTER THREE

1. Reflect on the inner meaning of Jesus' baptism. In what sense did this event call him to individuation? Can this call be heard in baptism today?

2. What do you find most difficult about standing against the group and being true to yourself? What are the benefits and liabilities of doing so? How might dream work and the imitation of Christ guide you?

3. What were the implications of Jesus placing compassion, not holiness, at the center of his faith? Why was this a threat to the purity system of the religion of his day, and what relevance does this have for modern Christians?

4. Do you find it helpful to think of the kingdom of God as the "spirituality of consciousness"? Discuss the gospel texts about the kingdom in this chapter as they relate to the idea of deepening one's inner awareness.

5. How do you respond to Neil Perry's choice of suicide instead of conformity in the movie *Dead Poets Society*? Is such a choice ever justified?

6. What specific experiences have you had of being a conformist or a nonconformist? How did you feel about yourself amid these experiences and what did you learn from them?

CHAPTER FOUR

1. Reflect on Gerald May's definitions of attachment and addiction quoted in this chapter. How do these definitions differ from or add to the biblical concept of sin? What spiritual resources offer hope of freedom from attachment and addiction?
2. Luke states that Jesus "was led by the Spirit in the wilderness." Does this suggest that at times the Spirit takes us into the wilderness for our own good? Are there other times when it's our own fault that we end up in the wilderness? What can we learn from Jesus' experience?
3. Why is it so important for us to be in touch with our *shadow*, as Jesus was? How do we know when we have begun our shadow work and are making progress? Do our dreams tell us anything?
4. When does the shadow have potential for good? Can you suggest any strategies for relating to people who have not begun their shadow work when you have begun yours?
5. Reflect on Jesus' three temptations. Do you agree or disagree that Jesus successfully resisted them because he disciplined his desire? Discuss each temptation and suggest ways we might follow him in discipline.
6. What insights from John of the Cross do you find helpful? Where can hope be found in "the dark night of the soul"?

CHAPTER FIVE

1. How do you respond to Don Marquis's statement about loneliness? Is this too extreme, or is the struggle against loneliness at the heart of all religion, art, and life?
2. Reflect on the personality flaws of the disciples and how Jesus dealt with them. What are the implications of the imitation of Christ for relationships? What about implications for the church as a healing community?

3. How might insights from depth psychology about egocentricity improve people's friendships and well-being? What does being "centered in God" mean in psychological terms?
4. What does the statement "centered people offer their friends the right blend of intimacy and space" say about having clear relationship boundaries of one's own and respecting the boundaries of others?
5. Using Parker Palmer's experience with depression as an example, discuss what people who are hurting need most. As a friend, when is it best just to listen and be a healing presence? When is it okay to help someone "fix" a problem?
6. Jesus said there is no greater love than "to lay down one's life for one's friends." Is it possible to lay down one's life and still take care of oneself? How can we guard against burnout and codependency?

CHAPTER SIX

1. In the Sermon on the Mount, Jesus said he came not to abolish the law but to fulfill it. Do you agree or disagree that integrative love fulfills the law's inner meaning?
2. What is the difference between legalism and creativity? What other sayings or parables of Jesus can you think of that illustrate this difference?
3. Does your experience confirm or deny the thesis of this chapter that aligning one's life with the inner spirit of the Sermon on the Mount nurtures contentment? In what sense was Jesus content or discontent, and what are the implications of imitating him?
4. What is the relationship between perfectionism and the shadow? How might doing one's shadow work reduce the pain that perfectionism causes?
5. Why is it important to have a strong theology of the cross when you fail to meet the requirements of the Sermon on the Mount? How do the concepts of atonement and imitation complement or contradict each other in the Christian life?
6. Reflect on the experience of Admiral Richard E. Byrd. What does this experience say to you about being "centered in God"?

CHAPTER SEVEN

1. The physical brokenness of a Roman centurion's servant is highlighted in Matthew 8. What other forms does brokenness take? Which of these do you identify with most, and how is Jesus a healer for you?
2. Nearly one-fifth of the Gospels is devoted to Jesus' healings and responses to them. This is the greatest emphasis given to one kind of experience except miracles in general. What is the significance of this? Should Christianity be therapeutic or doctrinal or both? How does the imitation of Christ inform your answer?
3. What is the difference between individualism and individuation? What are some behaviors associated with each? How might the good behaviors be encouraged and the bad ones avoided?
4. In what sense was Jesus whole and in what sense was he broken? How does his experience relate to ours? What does it mean to be a "wounded healer"?
5. Can seeking one's own wholeness become a selfish, narcissistic preoccupation? How might Fritz Kunkel's "We Psychology" help one avoid this?
6. What is the difference between happiness and wholeness? What is the role of grace in fostering the latter?

CHAPTER EIGHT

1. The storm at sea is used in this chapter as a metaphor for the problems of life. Reflect on Jung's idea of the hero's journey and, using the experience of Jesus and the disciples as an example, identify the differences between heroic and unheroic responses to your problems.
2. How do you respond to the idea of the hero's journey as an adventure? Is this idea too optimistic to be helpful in handling even the worst tragedies, or do you find it useful?
3. Mythologists have described a life crisis or a time of deep depression as "the Night-Sea Journey." What conditions must be present in order for these experiences to promote inner development?

4. A major theme in the story of the storm at sea is the necessity of faith amid crisis. What can we learn about the relationship between faith and centeredness by contrasting the response of Jesus with that of the disciples?
5. Have you ever made such a bad mistake that a situation exploded and left you totally unable to control the outcome? What does it mean to depend on grace in such situations?
6. Do you believe that "God is not only in the Big Picture but also in the details"? How might your dreams help you discern God's presence and guidance?

CHAPTER NINE

1. What are some examples of things that cannot be changed and must be accepted? Are there other things that we must not accept but must always seek to change?
2. How do you respond to Jesus' experience in the Garden of Gethsemane? What kind of inner growth is necessary before a person can really say to God "not what I want, but what you want"?
3. Does acceptance usually come all at once and stay, or does it come gradually and sometimes need to be reclaimed?
4. Reflect on Jung's statement about his patients who "were able to become reconciled to themselves, and thus were reconciled to adverse circumstances and events." What is the relationship between self-acceptance and one's ability to cope with life?
5. Why is it important to maintain a dialogue among Scripture, tradition, reason, and experience in the Christian life? How might this dialogue encourage spiritual growth, and how might an imbalance among these elements create problems?
6. "Life's goal is not to understand but to trust." Using Jesus' experience in Gethsemane as a reference point, consider whether or not you agree with this statement and why.

CHAPTER TEN

1. Do you think of the cross mostly as a means of atonement or as a moral example? Why is an integrative perspective

needed in the Christian life? What are the dangers of emphasizing either perspective and minimizing the other?

2. Reflect on the cross as a symbol of individuation. What role does inner suffering play in bringing the self fully into the light of consciousness?

3. Why is egocentricity antithetical to individuation? Do you agree or disagree that self-giving is essential to achieving individuation?

4. What comfort, if any, do you find in Christianity's great reversals—its celebration of poverty instead of wealth, weakness instead of strength, and so forth? When in your life have these reversals been most important to you?

5. Can self-giving be taken too far? What are some signs that this is happening, particularly in your dreams? Does it help to be aware of the difference between martyrdom and consciousness?

6. Do you find M. Scott Peck's definition of love helpful or unhelpful? Using the insights of this chapter as a point of reference, formulate your understanding of what it means to love.

CHAPTER ELEVEN

1. How do you tend to think about Christ's resurrection? Do you emphasize Easter more as a triumph over physical death or as a triumph over spiritual death within life? How might an integrative perspective that brings the resurrection hope to all experiences change you?

2. Do you agree or disagree with Jung that the Resurrection represents the triumph of "the greater personality in every individual"? In your opinion, is the category saved/unsaved essential to Christianity?

3. What does the idea of living in the "resurrection consciousness" mean to you? How can you measure the progress you are making in doing so, and what spiritual disciplines are necessary to maintain this progress?

4. Is there a difference between listening to your turmoil and listening to your soul? How do you know when you are listening and when you are not? Does paying attention to your dreams help?

5. How important is it that Jesus actually met with people after the Resurrection? Do these relationships have anything to teach today's Christians about what it means to be "Easter people?"
6. How does this chapter relate to the rest of the book? Consider the ways in which the integrative approach to Christianity has been helpful to you. What points can you criticize?

ACKNOWLEDGMENTS

I started this book in the fall of 1988, but in a deeper sense, I have been working on it all my life and will never finish it. No one is ever totally centered in God.

But I am profoundly grateful to numerous people who have helped me on this inward journey. One of them, John A. Sanford, a true mentor through his books on Christianity and Jungian psychology, wrote the Foreword. Others are mentioned in this book, though occasionally their names have been changed and their stories scrambled to protect their anonymity. Some of them I have never met, but I feel a kinship with them through their writings.

One of these was the African American theologian and former dean of Marsh Chapel at Boston University, Howard Thurman. His book *Jesus and the Disinherited* (Richmond, Indiana: Friends United Press, 1949), which I first read in a course with Professor John H. Cartwright at Boston University, introduced me to the "religion of Jesus," an idea that underlies my thoughts about Jesus' spirituality. Another of my favorite authors, Lewis B. Smedes, inspired the structure of the chapter titles and the emphasis on grace with his book *How Can It Be All Right When Everything Is All Wrong?*

Members of my congregation of Central Baptist Church have been wonderfully supportive of me as a pastor and writer. They encouraged me in many intangible and invaluable ways as this project progressed, as did the Rhode Island Friends of Jung, whose monthly discussions have never failed to stimulate my thinking.

I offer special thanks to Marie Cantlon, whose astute editorial guidance helped me improve the manuscript in the early stages. She taught me a lot in a short time about how to write a book and became a friend in the process. I am grateful to Diana Litterick for reading the manuscript and giving me feedback. Mike Burch and Lou Quetel, both true soul mates, shared my enthusiasm for this project and provided constant inspiration as I worked on it.

Ron Klug, director of publishing at Augsburg Books, was the right editor for me at the right time. I thank him for his personal warmth and wise counsel all along the way.

The person I respect, admire, and love most of all is my wife, Carol. I am forever in her debt for believing in me as a minister and a writer, for sharing with me the journey of life and faith that led to this book, and especially for modeling what it means to be centered in God and for calling me back to that center when I stray.

EVAN DRAKE HOWARD, 1995

If you wish to contact the author, please write to him at the address below:

Evan Drake Howard
117 Wilcox Avenue
Pawtucket, RI 02860-5760